ARCHITECTURE

images
Publishing

NeoArchitecture

24H

ARCHITECTURE

Published in Australia in 2007 by
The Images Publishing Group Pty Ltd
ABN 89 059 734 431
6 Bastow Place, Mulgrave, Victoria 3170, Australia
Tel: +61 3 9561 5544 Fax: +61 3 9561 4860
books@imagespublishing.com
www.imagespublishing.com

Copyright © The Images Publishing Group Pty Ltd 2007
The Images Publishing Group Reference Number: 730

The National Library of Australia
Cataloguing-in-Publication data:

Lammers, Maartje.
24H Architecture.

ISBN 978 1 92074 484 7 (hbk)

1. 24H Architecture (firm). 2. Architecture – Netherlands.
3. Space (Architecture) – Netherlands. 4. Sustainable
architecture – Netherlands. I. Zeisser, Boris. II. Title.

720.9492

Edited by Janelle McCulloch

Designed by The Graphic Image Studio Pty Ltd, Mulgrave, Australia
www.tgis.com.au

Digital production by Splitting Image Colour Studio Pty Ltd, Australia
Printed by Sing Cheong Printing Co., Ltd, Hong Kong

CONTENTS

INTRODUCTION
SIGNS OF CHANGE

Rotterdam. A city that prides itself on a spirit of experimentation in building. It's a reputation that reaches well beyond the country's borders and into the international marketplace, and in fact has become so widespread that the city has now become a destination for aesthetically driven travellers in search of contemporary architecture as well as young designers in search of experience at one of a number of Rotterdam's renowned architecture firms. The city has also become a place of preference for architects seeking to establish their own design practices.

One of these emerging architectural firms is 24H architecture, headed by Maartje Lammers and Boris Zeisser. Partners in life as well as in practice, the couple chose 01-01-01 as an appropriate date to open their office doors for the first time. For the time being, these doors are located inside the Van Nelle Factory, an icon of Dutch Functionalist design from the 1930s that has become home to an innovative crop of start-up firms in the city's creative sector.

That Maartje Lammers and Boris Zeisser should have chosen to operate from this paragon of functionalist design may be little other than a matter of expediency. After all, the interiors do make for agreeable workspaces. But the setting nonetheless provides a fitting, albeit unintentional, counterpoint to the work of the designers. The Van Nelle factory is as rigorous and rational as the work of 24H architecture is expressive. Architecture stripped to the bare essentials versus architecture strongly flavoured by embellishment. Recently the firm moved to their new location, an historic school that is more appropriate to 24H.

Such an emphatic style does not emerge overnight. It is the expression of an attitude that has been evolving since the firm's inception. And no doubt the process must have started way before this time when its two founders were working for some of most prominent architectural offices in the Netherlands – Boris Zeisser at the office of (EEA) Erick van Egeraat, Maartje Lammers at OMA, Mecanoo and EEA. Into their own practice they have taken with them something of the analytical power of OMA as well as the baroque exuberance of van Egeraat.

The firm's philosophy of shunning the straightforward and the severe is something of an exception in the Dutch architectural scene. The reductive palette favoured by so many of the country's designers – a hangover from the decades in which a sober functionalism held the country hostage – certainly finds no echo in the work of this office. If anything, Lammers and Zesser seem to positively rebel against the mentality that thriftiness is a virtue. Their aim is to instil spaces and places with a personality and warmth that's often lacking in the built environment. They do not buy into the philosophy that sparseness is better and excess is surfeit. In fact, in 24H's case, excess is more a matter of expressiveness. Lammers and Zeisser create designs that don't merge meekly into their surroundings but instead stand out proudly and conspicuously. Embedded within these designs are fragments of tactile and visual richness – a succession of novel details – that inspire affection in us vis-à-vis our surroundings and offer us an eventful experience. How else can one explain the star-spangled ceilings of the pouch-like interview rooms hollowed out of the innards of the sculptural fish that stretches across the interior of the Rotterdam business school, like some aquatic creature washed up on the shore? Or the skin of cedar shingles that wraps the biomorphic body of the fairytale-style holiday home deep in the Swedish woods? Or even the multi-jointed limbs attached to the ribcage of the beach pavilion, which slides along the pier, in and out of the water like a waddling crustacean?

Such allusions to the world of living organisms are no surprise given that **evolution** is one of four themes that manifest themselves in differing proportions and combinations in the projects presented in this book. Evolution is used to denote the capacity of buildings to adapt in response to needs that change according to the conditions of the moment, the hour of the day, or the season of the year. This is a facet of design insufficiently explored in architecture but immensely significant in other fields of design. It also explains the allusion to the time in the name of 24H's office.

A second recurring theme is **sensibility**: the desire to infuse buildings with a richness of detail that endears them to their occupants. The desire to make grand statements and engage in conceptual games often consumes architects to the point where they are blinded to the simple reality that a building stands or falls (figuratively speaking) on the strength of its details. The works gathered in this book are evidence of a heightened sensitivity to the communicative power of the architectural detail. We see it in the Hoofddorp apartment block where strips of gold-coloured anodised aluminium sheeting adorned with a leaf motif weave in and out of the façade. The resulting irregular rhythm not only gives every apartment a unique appearance but also forms a portal to the row of houses at the rear.

A third theme is what Lammers and Zeisser call **landshape**, an umbrella term that encompasses not only how new elements are inserted into the surrounding landscape but also how environmental issues and

sustainable building technologies influence design. Such a close relationship with landscape is no surprise in a country where the very landscape itself is a man-made entity that is moulded and remoulded to meet the needs of a society in evolution. The Netherlands enjoys a rich tradition in allowing patterns of settlement and patterns of landscape to extend easily from one to the other. And that tradition is apparent in the folded ground plane of the Haarlemmermeer primary school, which takes its cue from the neighbouring ribbon development. In this school, inclined roof gardens extend over the classroom wings to emphasise the close ties between building and nature.

Close ties also describe how these four themes interact with one another. Those same roof gardens, for instance, can also be read as an illustration of the fourth and final theme: **event**. It is by far the most abstract of the themes, since it doesn't refer to the physical substance of architecture – to built matter – but rather that which architectural facilitates. Architecture itself, after all, is of no significance unless it becomes the setting against which everyday activity can flourish. We see an awareness of this fact in the coat of bristling quills that turns an Amsterdam pumping house into the architectural equivalent of a porcupine. This façade does more than give a building a recognisable form. It also functions as a climbing frame for children and as a gigantic nesting place for birds. It is, in essence, a stage set for events that will one day be enacted.

These four themes crop up in different combinations and proportions in each project, increasing or decreasing in importance in response to the nature of the design task. Indeed, their exact mixture is as unique to each project as a fingerprint is to a person. And while the designs presented here are all related to one another, each individual project has a personality that sets it apart from its siblings. To scan the portfolio of 24H architecture is to share the designers' enthusiasm for enriching everyday structures and spaces with qualities whose potential is undervalued by many architects. These works, some built and most imagined, unlock a world in which architecture becomes sensual, buildings acquire a face, and details warm the spirit – a counterpoint to that other architectural world in which chilly functionality rules. The works presented in this book are proof that a change of climate is occurring. Even though one building is constructed entirely of ice, a thaw has definitely set in.

CLIENT: Zeisser, Sweden
DESIGN TEAM: Boris Zeisser, Maartje Lammers with Olav Bruin, Fieke
Poelman, Sabrina Kers, Jeroen ter Haar, Séverine Kas,
Ingrid Owens, Ruben Bergambagt
DESIGN: 2001–2002
CONSTRUCTION: 2001–2004
FLOOR AREA: 54–72 square metres
BUILDING COSTS: €80,000

Dragspelhuset Summer House

LAKE ÖVRE GLA, SWEDEN

This project was an extension to an original cabin dating from the 1800s, located on the shore of Lake Övre Gla in the Glaskogen Nature Reserve in Sweden. According to Swedish building regulations, construction along lakeshores is prohibited unless it is an extension to an existing building. Other restrictions included a maximum floor area and a distance of 4.5 metres to the stream that forms part of the site boundary.

To make maximum use of these potentially restrictive building regulations, 24H designed an extension to the cabin that could evolve over time. The building can literally adjust itself to its environment depending on weather conditions, seasons or the number of occupants. The extension unfurls like a butterfly: during the winter it's a cocoon, compact with a double skin against the cold; during the summer the building can change its form or, like a butterfly, unfold its wings for extra shelter during rainy days.

When the space is at its largest, and those residing in the cabin are living above the falling water of the stream, the senses are aroused to their sharpest.

The organic shape of the house blends naturally into the setting of the rough forest. The traditional roofing solution (*stickor* or shingled roof), which was common in Sweden many years ago, was reused here in a contemporary way. Canadian cedarwood was chosen for the *stickor* because it requires no maintenance. In due time the wood will fade to an elegant grey shade, fitting seamlessly into the rough rocky forest landscape. Creating the cabin extension this way will ensure that the house will camouflage itself during the absence of its inhabitants, and settle into the landscape. ■

1　*Night view of front*
2　*Extended longitudinal section*

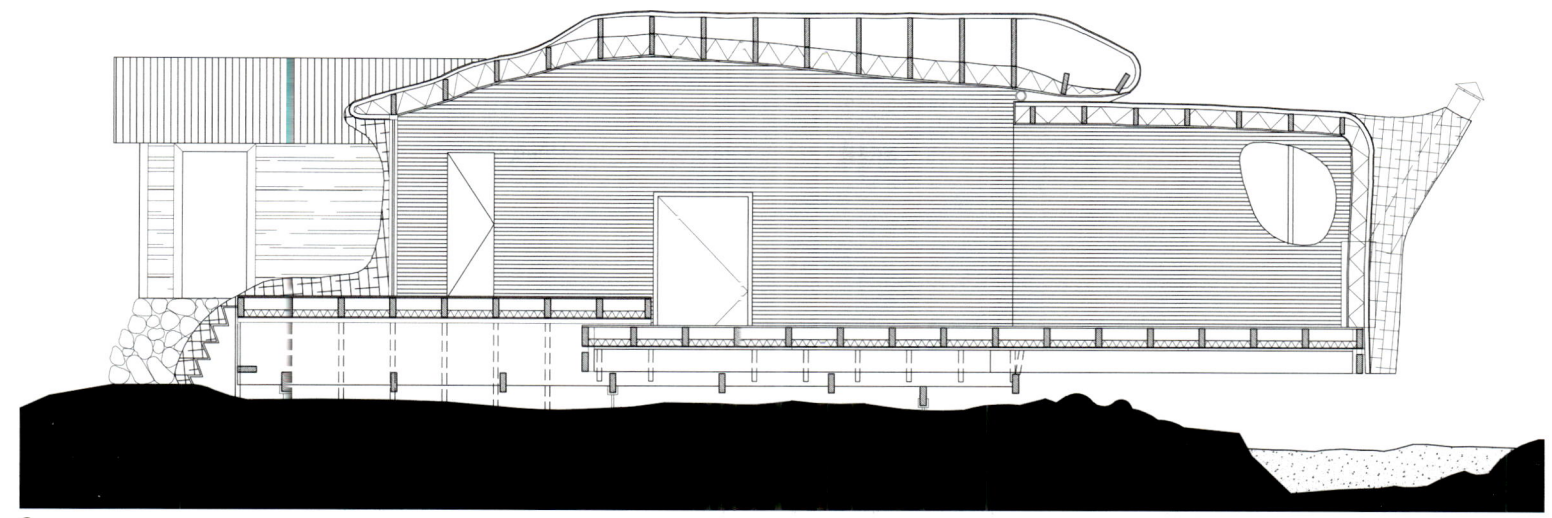

2

3

4

3 *Night view*
4 *Extended view of front façade*
5 *Exterior bathroom*
6 *Living room*
7 *Axonometric view of structure*

10

5

6

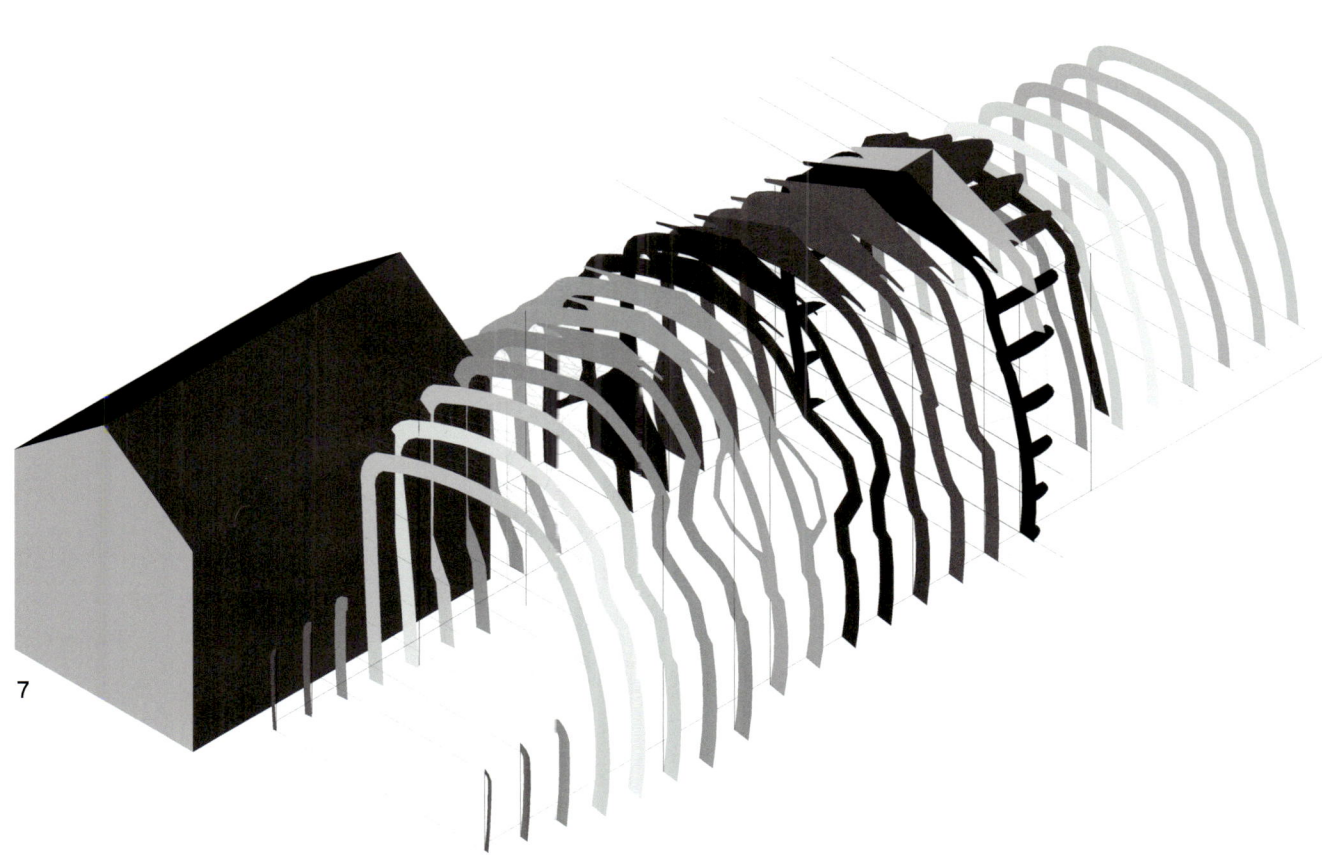

7

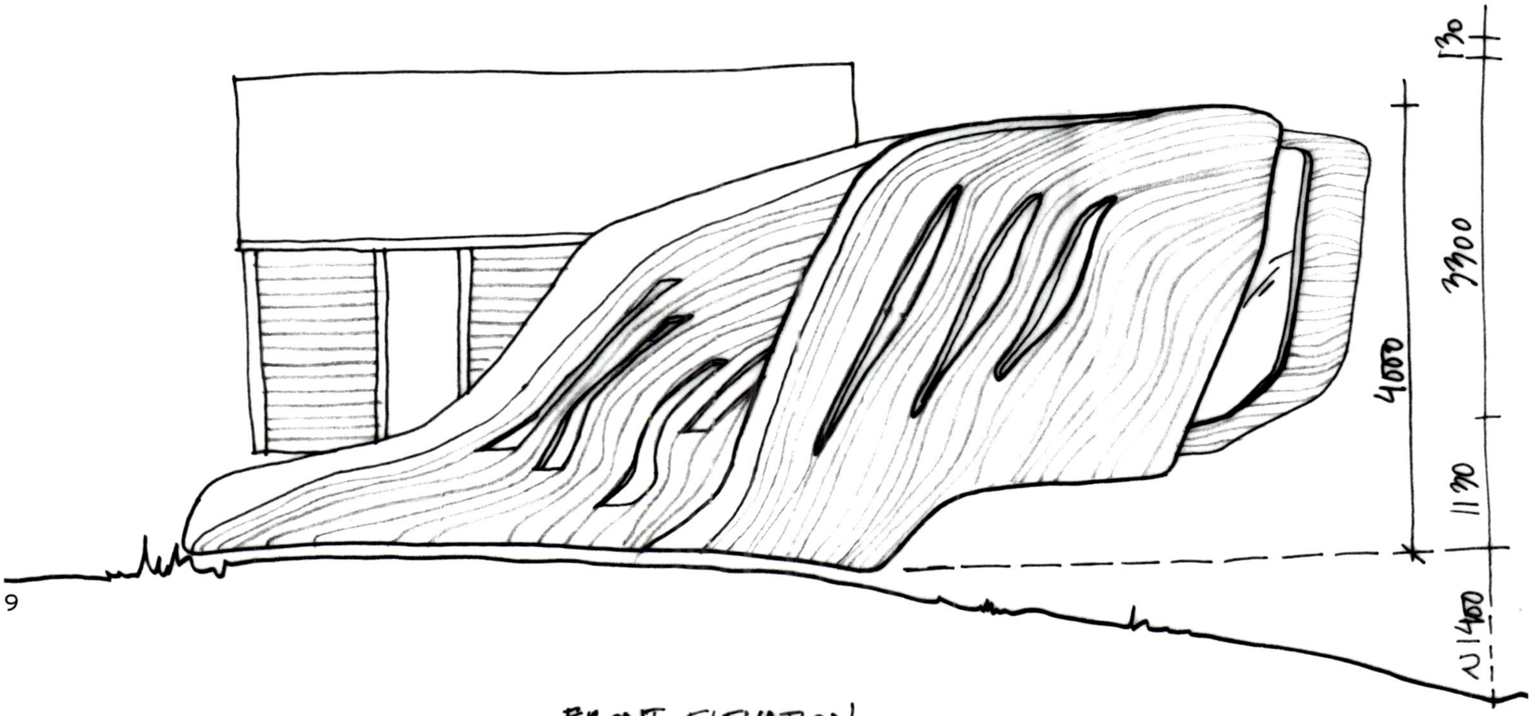
130
3300
4000
1190
~1400
FRONT ELEVATION
FROM ÖVREGA

9

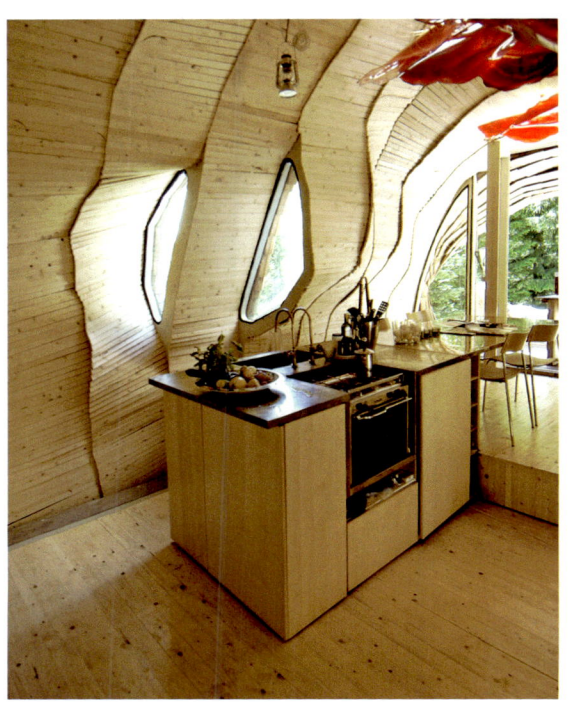

10

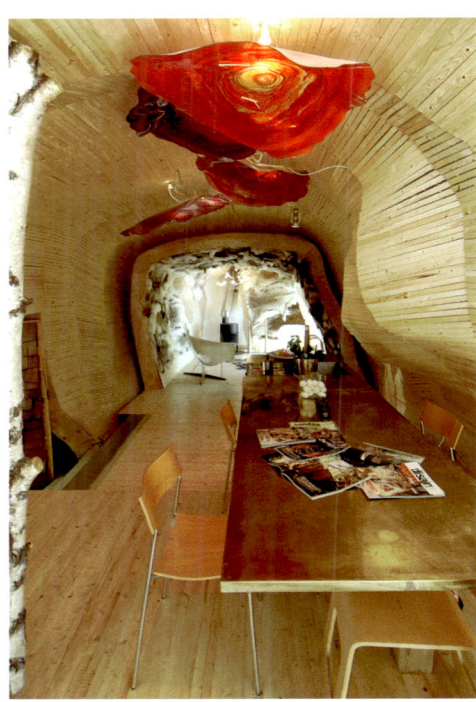

11

8 *Kitchen windows*
9 *Original sketch*
10 *Kitchen counter*
11 *Dining table*

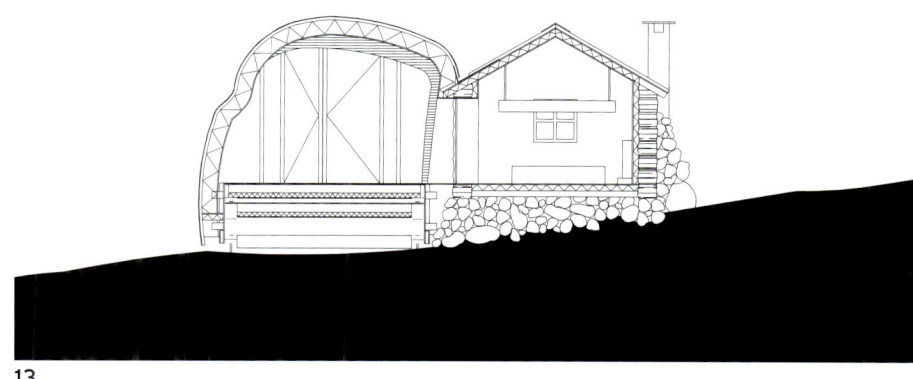

13

12 *Living room features reindeer skin on walls and ceiling*
13 *Cross section through original cabin*
21 *Detail of 'eye', seen from inside*

15

14

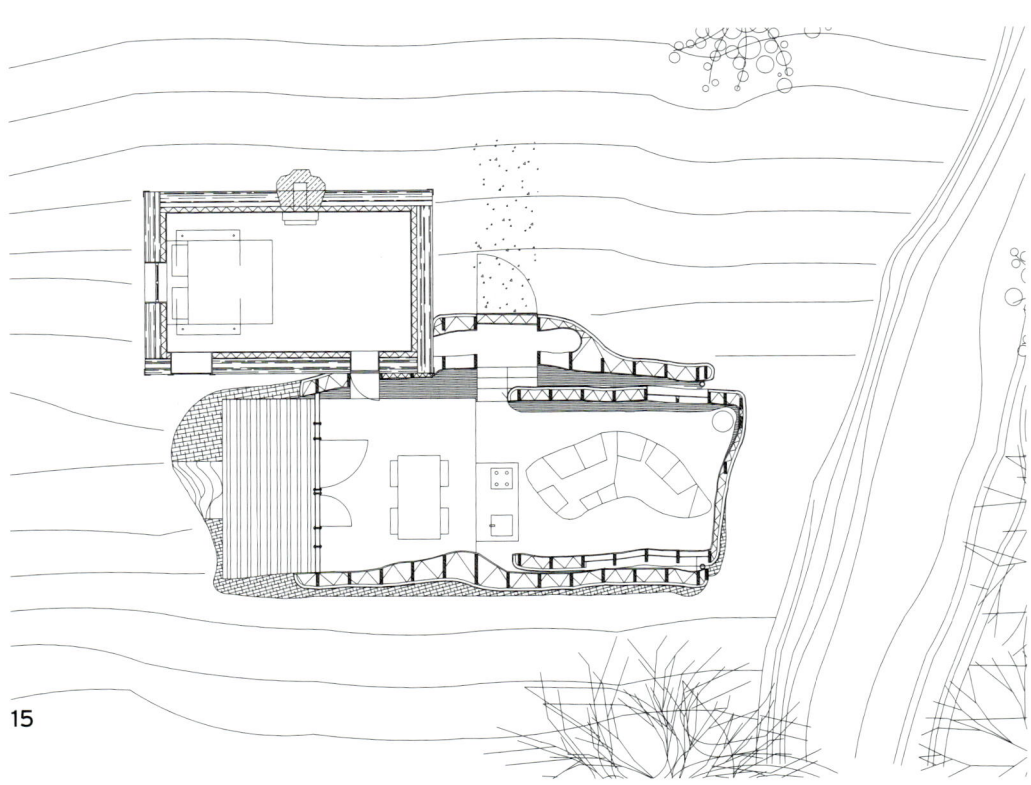

15 *Floor plan*
16 *Floor plan of building extended*
Opposite *View of lake*

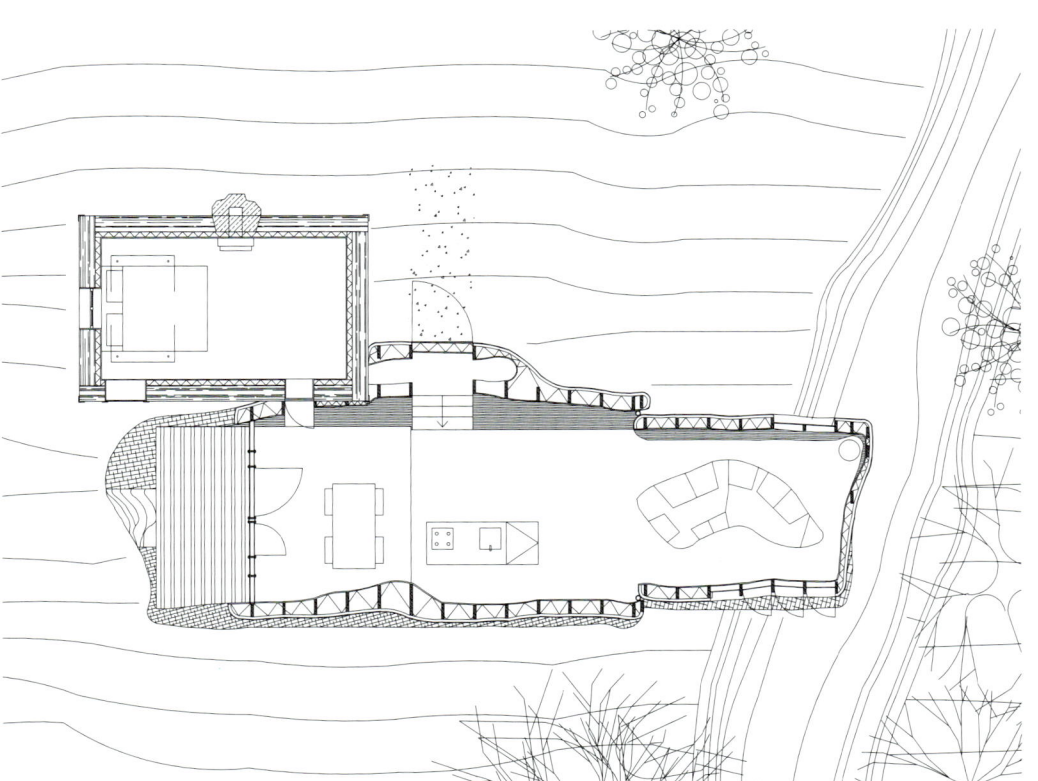

CLIENT: Ymere Amsterdam, The Netherlands
DESIGN TEAM: Boris Zeisser, Maartje Lammers with Gerben Vos, Heleen Bothof, Sabrina Kers, Jeroen ter Haar, Ingrid Owens
DESIGN: 2001–2002
CONSTRUCTION: 2003
FLOOR AREA: 4500 square metres
BUILDING COSTS: €3.6 million

Getsewoud Housing

NIEUW VENNEP, THE NETHERLANDS

In the urban plan for the 'Vinex' area of Getsewoud, Nieuw Vennep, the site forms the entrance of a specific part of a newly built housing area. From an urban point of view, 24H's contributory plan accentuated this entrance, using the soundwave as metaphor. This way, the rows of housing, with their variety of heights, create an entrance that essentially forms a 'gate'.

One part of the assignment consisted of a block that encompassed nine houses for young people. The façade of these youngsters' dwellings contains horizontal curved stripes with areas of classical bond brickwork and more random bond brickwork. The wooden window frames peek out of the brickwork, determining the façade's view.

The other part of the project required two blocks of social housing, each containing 18 apartments. The façade of these blocks is made of horizontal stripes of glass and precast purple concrete panels with a corrugated texture. The pattern, inspired by the wad-tile made by ceramics artist Babs Haenen, was designed using three-dimensional computer programs and, later, CNC spindles, which produced the moulds for the panels. So it was possible to realise this panelling exactly and precisely, with minimum technical effort. ∎

1 *Side façade*
2 *Entrance*
3 *Detail*

1

2

3

4

4 *3D diagram of concrete shape*
5 *Concept sketch*
6 *View from the balcony*

5

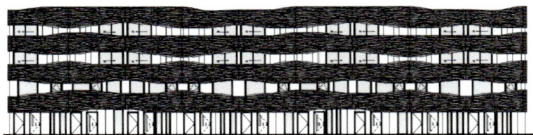

7

8

7 *Façades*
8 *Urban space*
9 *Balcony*
10 *Detail of façade*

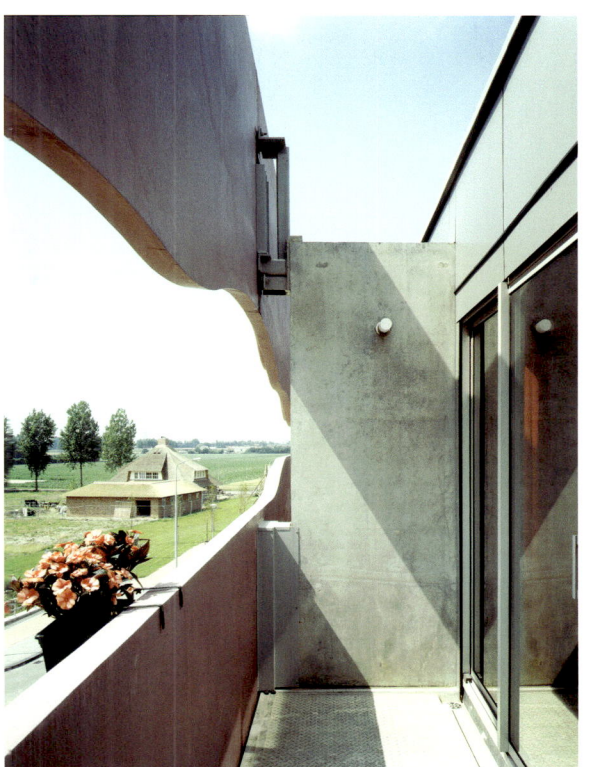

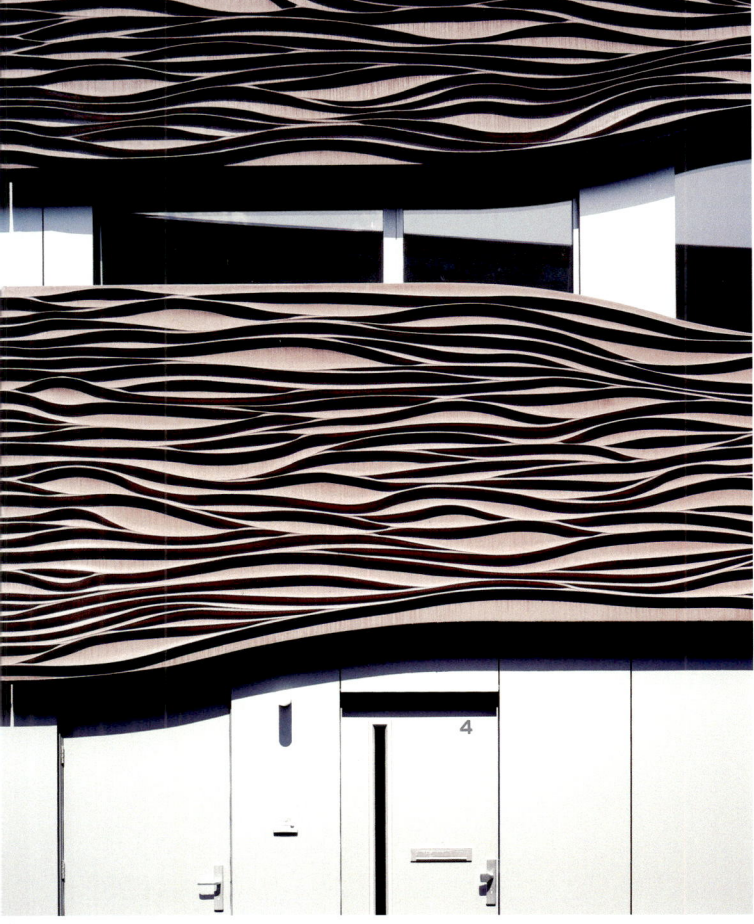

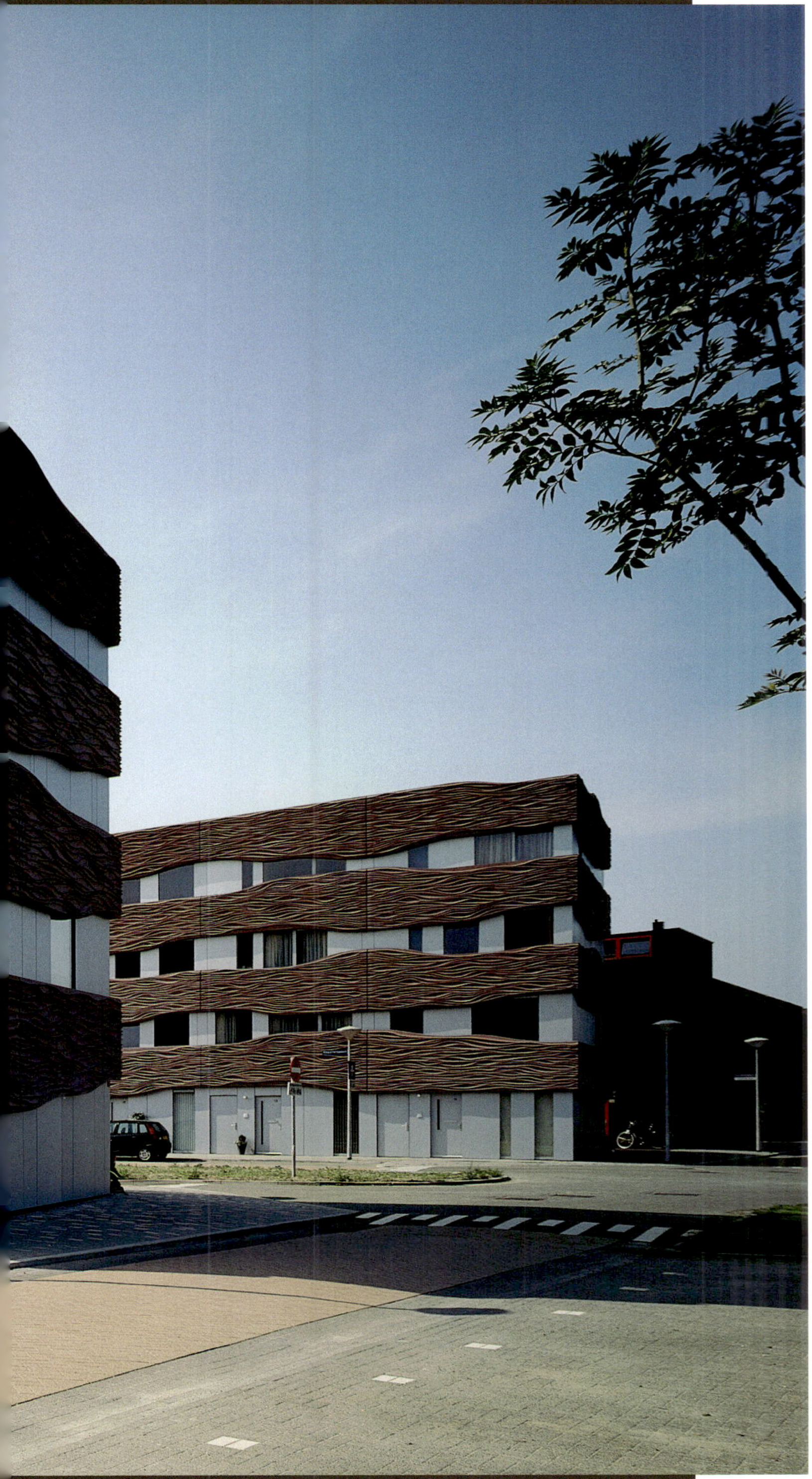

9

10

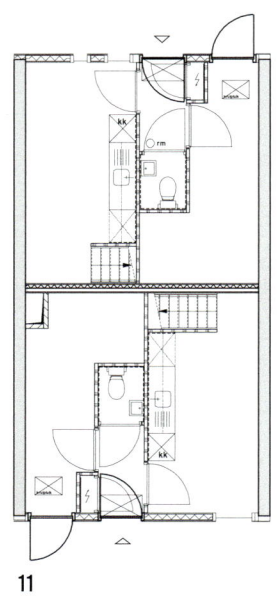
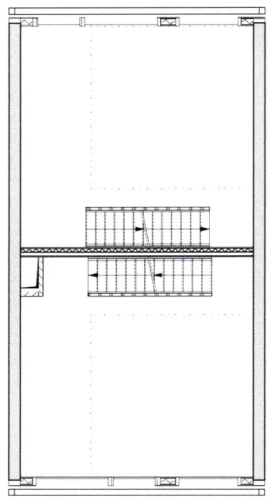
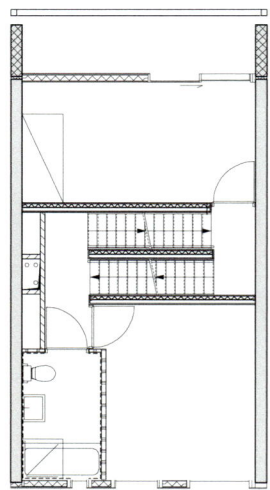
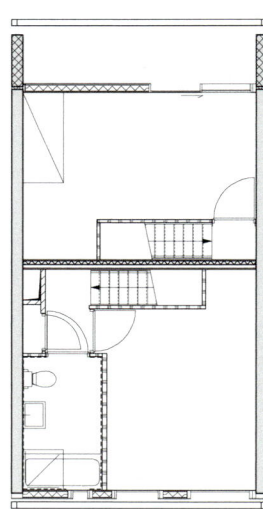

11

12

13

11 *Apartment floor plans*
12 *Façade of main block*
13 *Entrance façade of youngsters' dwellings*

CLIENT: Ichthus Academy, Rotterdam, The Netherlands
DESIGN TEAM: Boris Zeisser, Maartje Lammers with Jeroen ter Haar, Heleen Bothof, Sabrina Kers, Severine Kas, Gerben Vos and Ingrid Owens
DESIGN: 2001
CONSTRUCTION: 2001
FLOOR AREA: 1800 square metres
BUILDING COSTS: €680,000

Ichthus Academy
ROTTERDAM, THE NETHERLANDS

1

2

A proposal was made to design a temporary interior for one of the departments of the Ichthus Academy, located in the former Ned Lloyd building on the Zalmhaven in Rotterdam.

This department of the college – an educational institute for undergraduate and postgraduate studies – was translated into a modern facility with a refreshingly contemporary interior through a design that incorporates flexibility, colours and the use of materials to differentiate it from the other offices in the main building, as well as meet the wishes and needs of its young users.

The classrooms, administration and ancillary spaces are all anchored to existing cores, shafts or columns, thus breaking up the awkward scale of the original office space into a series of now-legible units, or clusters.

The identities of these clusters are illustrated by ribbon-like outer walls, which sweep up gracefully and wrap themselves around the academic spaces while also providing seating areas outside classrooms.

Digital prints depicting brightly coloured faces and leaves are blown up beyond recognition and cover the tilted walls of the four classrooms, with subtle variations in colour defining the character of each.

Between each of the clusters, the circulation spaces expand and contract with renewed flexibility; their flow only interrupted by the lighting concealed in vertical panels of translucent perspex.

In the central foyer, which separates the public area from staff rooms and other administration services, there is a 'sculptural fish' that contains several meeting rooms within its body. Like a carcass of some creature from the deep washed up onto shore, this fish is made of a timber skeleton and

1 *Outside skin of 'sculptural fish'*
2 *Staff room*
3 *Tail of fish*

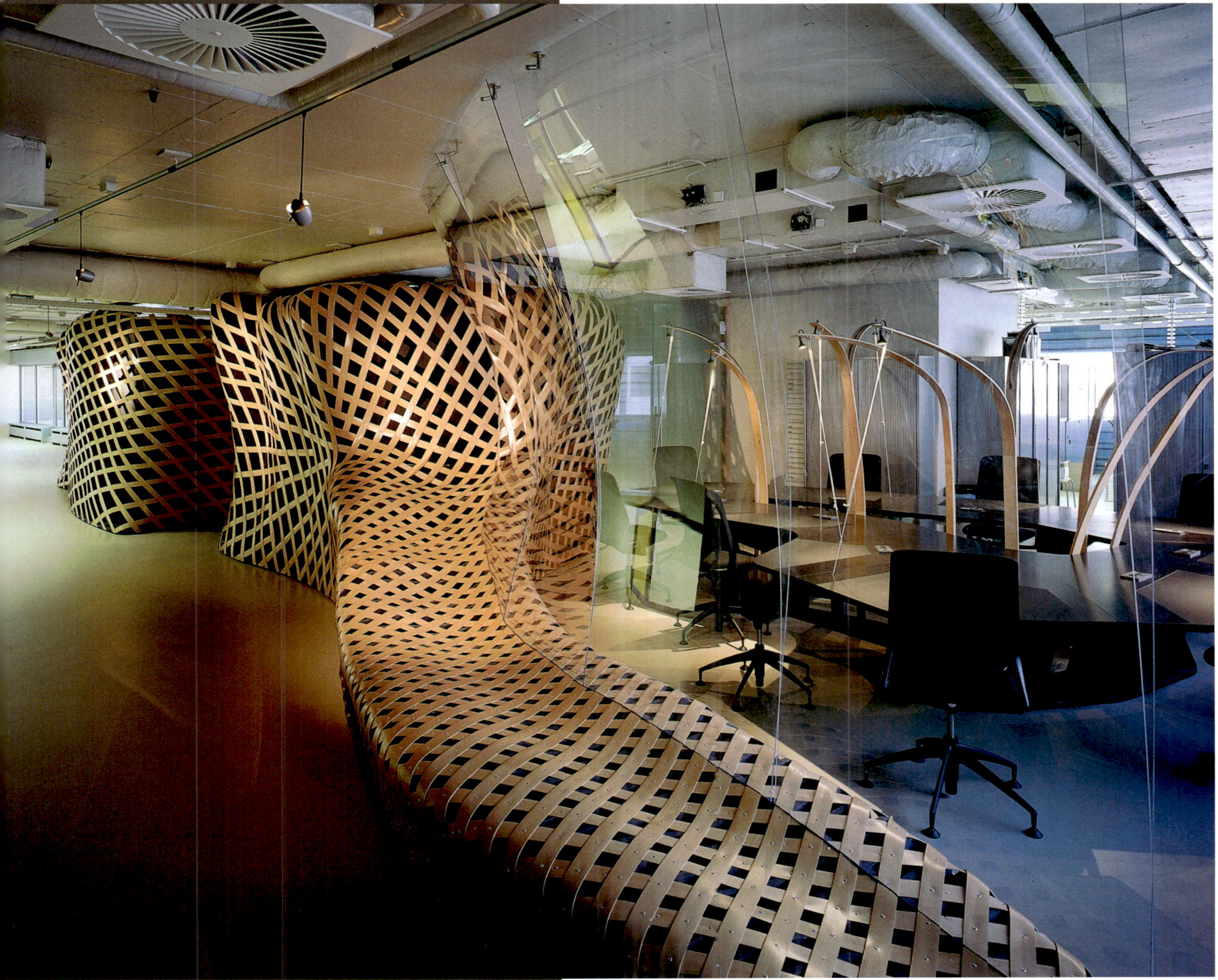

covered with a wickerwork of interwoven beech wood strips. Its tail tapers into a public bench near the coffee machine and separates the student area from the staff room behind.

The new design for Ichthus Academy successfully accommodated not only the classrooms and flow-through areas but several meeting rooms, public seating, an innovative 'entrance tunnel' to the administration spaces and even a view from the staff room to the foyer. ∎

4

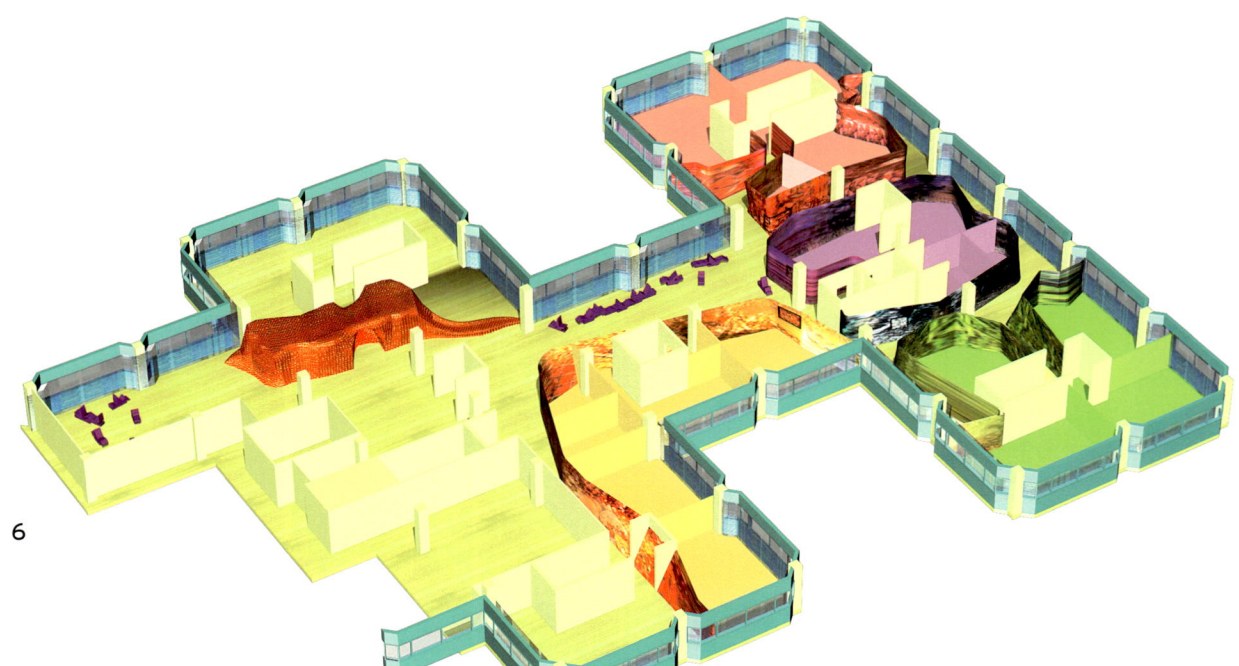

5

6

7

4 Concept rendering
5 Wallpaper
6 Axonometric view
7 Fish tapering into bench
8 Student lounge

8

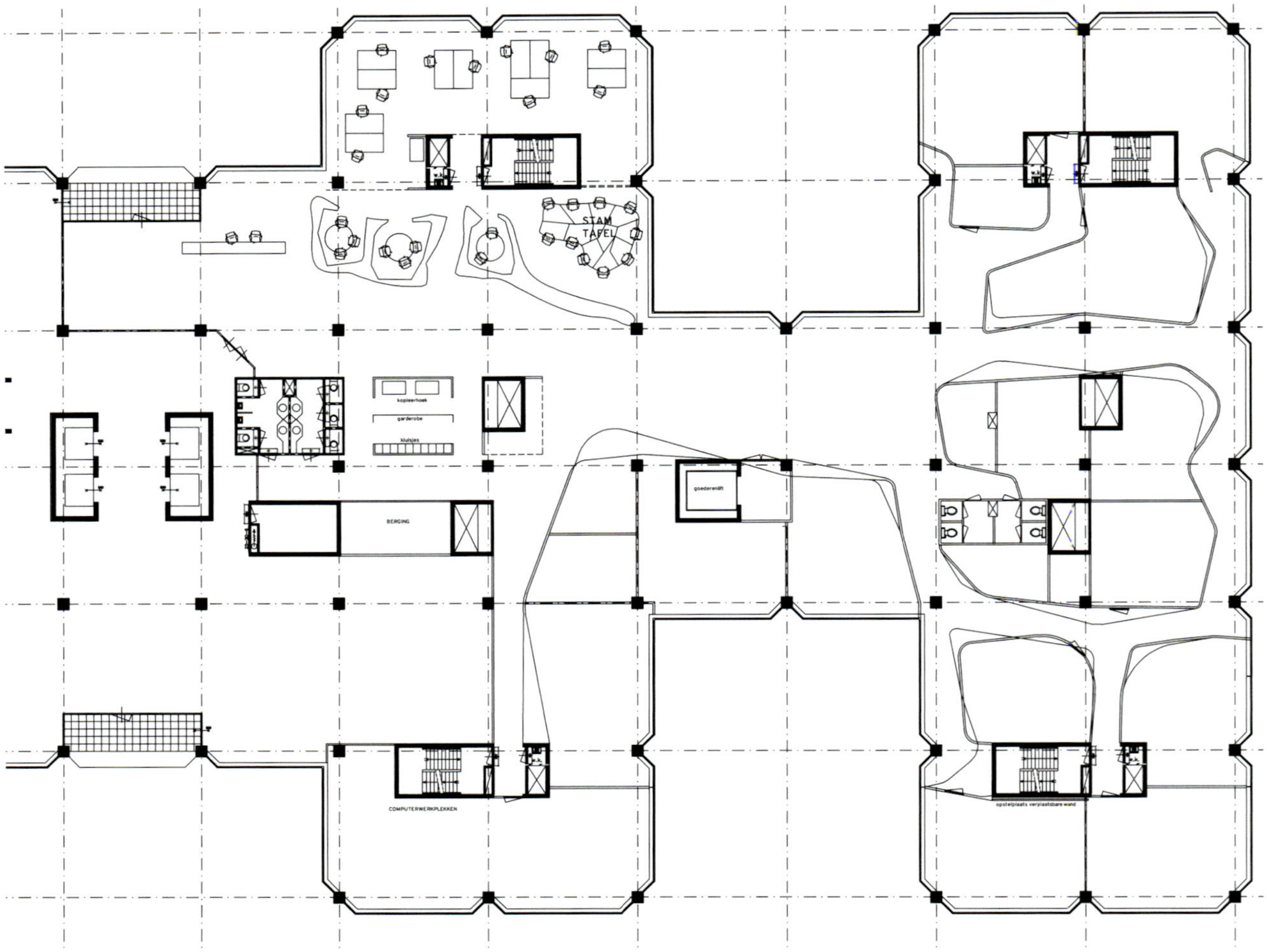
STAM
TAFEL
kopieerhoek
garderobe
kluisjes
BERGING
goederenlift
COMPUTERWERKPLEKKEN
opstelplaats verplaatsbare wand

9

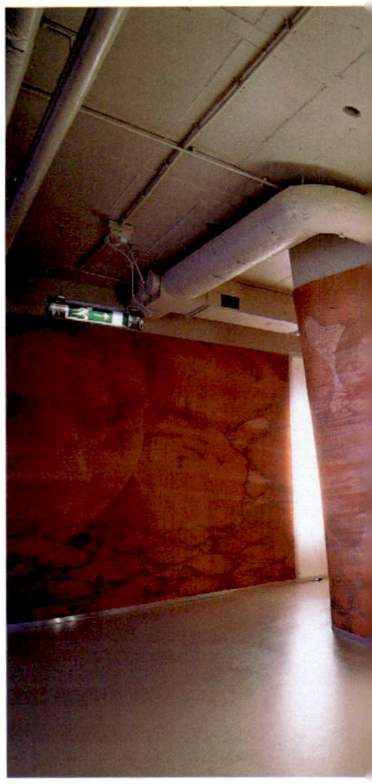

12

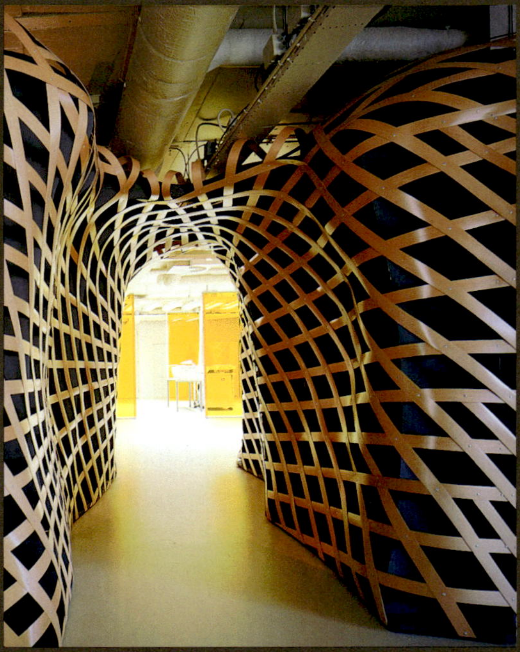

10

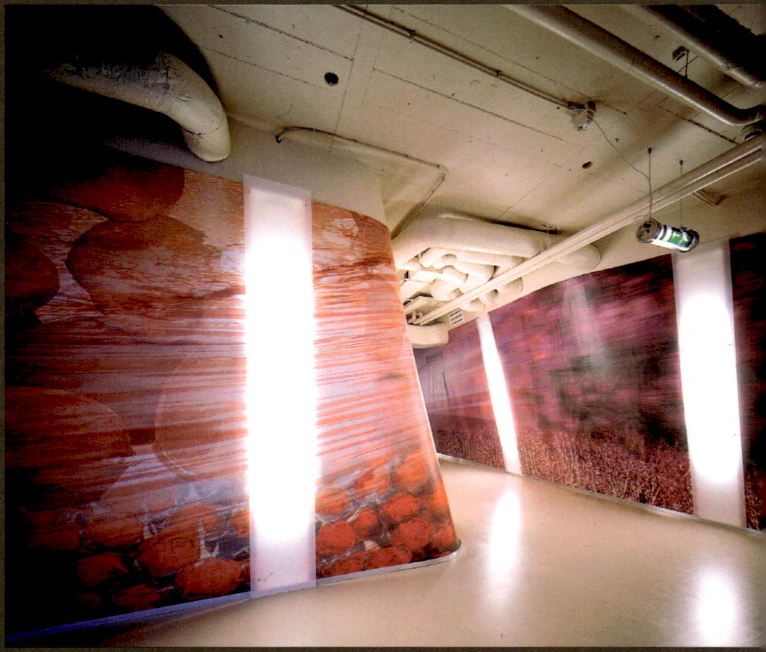

11

9   *Floor plan*
10 *Entrance tunnel to administration*
11–13 *Circulation space*
14 *Expanded circulation space becomes foyer*

31

13

14

CLIENT: Böblinger Baugesellschaft, Böblingen, Germany
DESIGN TEAM: Boris Zeisser, Maartje Lammers with Jeroen Ter Haar,
                Amelie Kaltenbach, Olav Bruin, Fieke Poelman
DESIGN: 2002 (competition)
FLOOR AREA: 4500 square metres
BUILDING COSTS: €7.6 million

Multifunctional Building

BÖBLINGEN, GERMANY

The design for the Schlossberg, the 'castle hill' in the centre of the south German city of Böblingen was designed to create a spectacular icon, a monument of the future that also intertwined seamlessly with the existing city.

The separate fabrics of the urban squares on either side of the hill, the *marktplatz* and the *postplatz*, are gradually being knitted together through growth. When they eventually meet, they will transform the area into one with a vibrant new urban texture. With this new design, this texture will be a brilliant façade of glass, which will form a crystal-clear new centrepiece for the city.

The underlying structure of this dazzling symbol for modernity is a two-dimensional base that evolves into a stunning three-dimensional volume that forms the building. Within this, an innovative design allows the building to be used as a whole, or as separate volumes to accommodate the diverse program offered by the museum, day care, city hall, restaurant and community centre. At once independent and yet joined by both the underlying fabric of the building and the urban life of the city, these volumes are connected by an impressive hall on the first level, which also serves as a the dramatic entrance leading visitors from the public world to a private one.

This new building is presented as a landmark within its environment, but also forms a flawless union with the structure of the city. It stands with dignity beside the existing church building while stopping short from dominating the environment. In short, it gives the city a new identity while forming a fautless merger with the much-loved fabric of Böblingen. ∎

1   *Cityscape*
2   *Aerial view of castle hill*
Opposite *Rendering*

4

5

6

7

8

4 *Model*
5 *Façade from* Marktplatz
6 *Façade from city wall*
7 *Façade from* Postplatz
8 *View from city centre*

9

36

10

11

12

13

14

CLIENT: Vizona, Amsterdam
DESIGN TEAM: Boris Zeisser, Maartje Lammers with Heleen Bothof
DESIGN: 2002
FLOOR AREA: 60 square metres

Shop Concept

VIZONA STORE, AMSTERDAM, THE NETHERLANDS

A concept was developed for the retail shop out-fitter Vizona for a series of fashion shops designed for the youth market.

The shop is to be centered by a "catwalk" runway, which shapes the entrance, and then, as it progress through the store, transforms into changing rooms.

This catwalk plays a dual role in the store, serving both the shopper and Vizona. The customers use the catwalk to view themselves while trying on clothes, while at the same time the overall "look" of the runway gives Vizona a unique atmosphere and energy. Other browser or those waiting for friends in the change room can further enjoy the "fashion show"-style atmosphere by occupying one of the integrated seating elements along the catwalk.

The surroundings of the catwalk are made of neutral materials, so all attention is focused solely on the catwalk and the clothes. ∎

1 *Detailed plan*
2 *Concept plan*
3 *Rendering*
4 *Concept sketch red carpet*

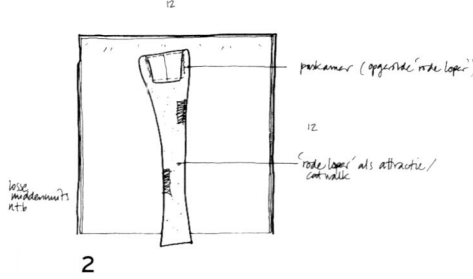

2

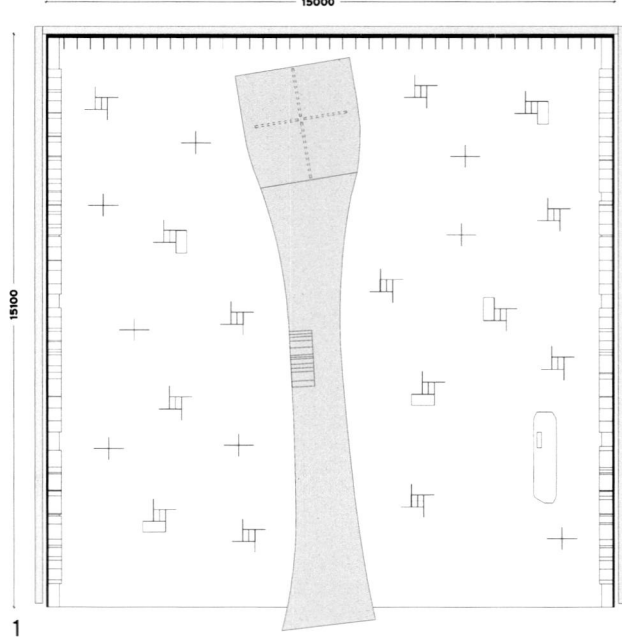

1

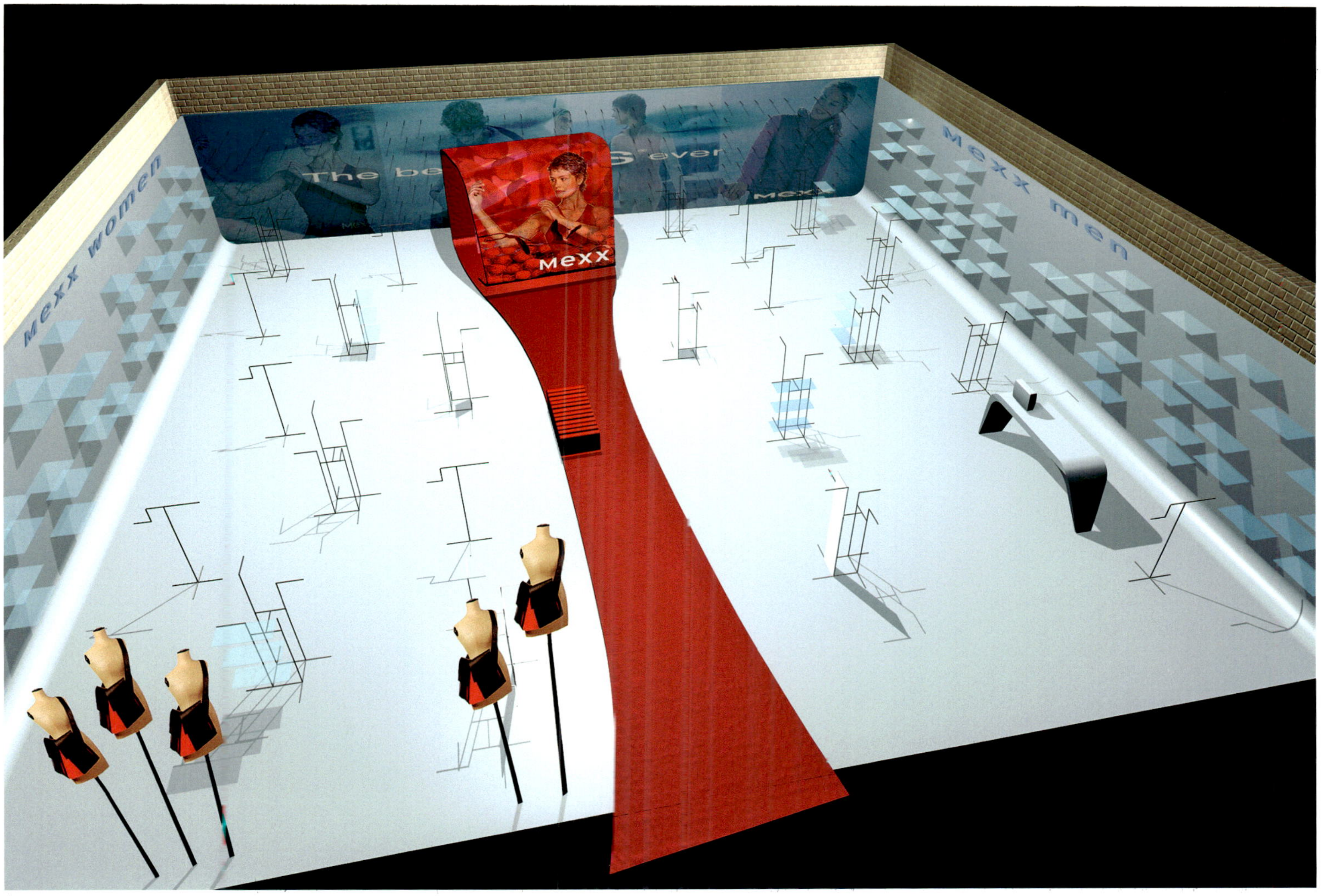

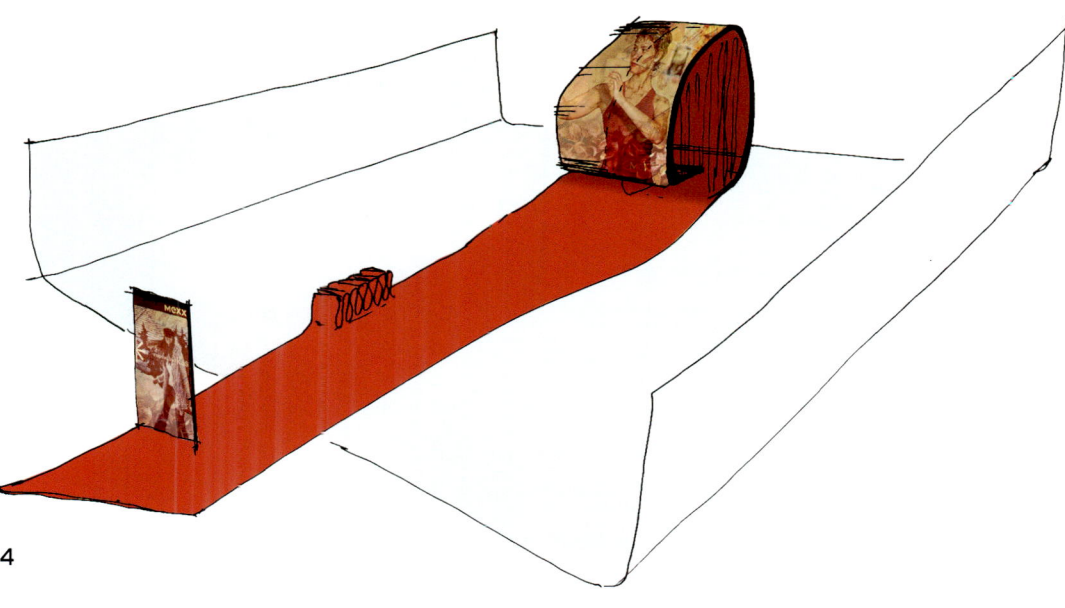

3

4

mexx women
mexx

5

VERLICHTING D.M.V. SPOTS
* SPIEGEL *
STALEN STRIP H.O.H 400MM
(2zijde DUIGEN)
GEPRINTE DOEK (VERTICAL VISION)
OP STRIPS BUIGPLEKS
HOUTEN SCHEGGEN
SPIEGELKLEM
HOOGPOLIG TAPIJT
RODE LOPER
OPEN !
ONDERSTEUNING
(OOK) OP TREK BELAST
GIETVLOER
ONDERVLOER
VARIABELE MAAT AFH.
VAN GROOTTE VAN WINKEL
HOOGTE 2.200 m

6

2560

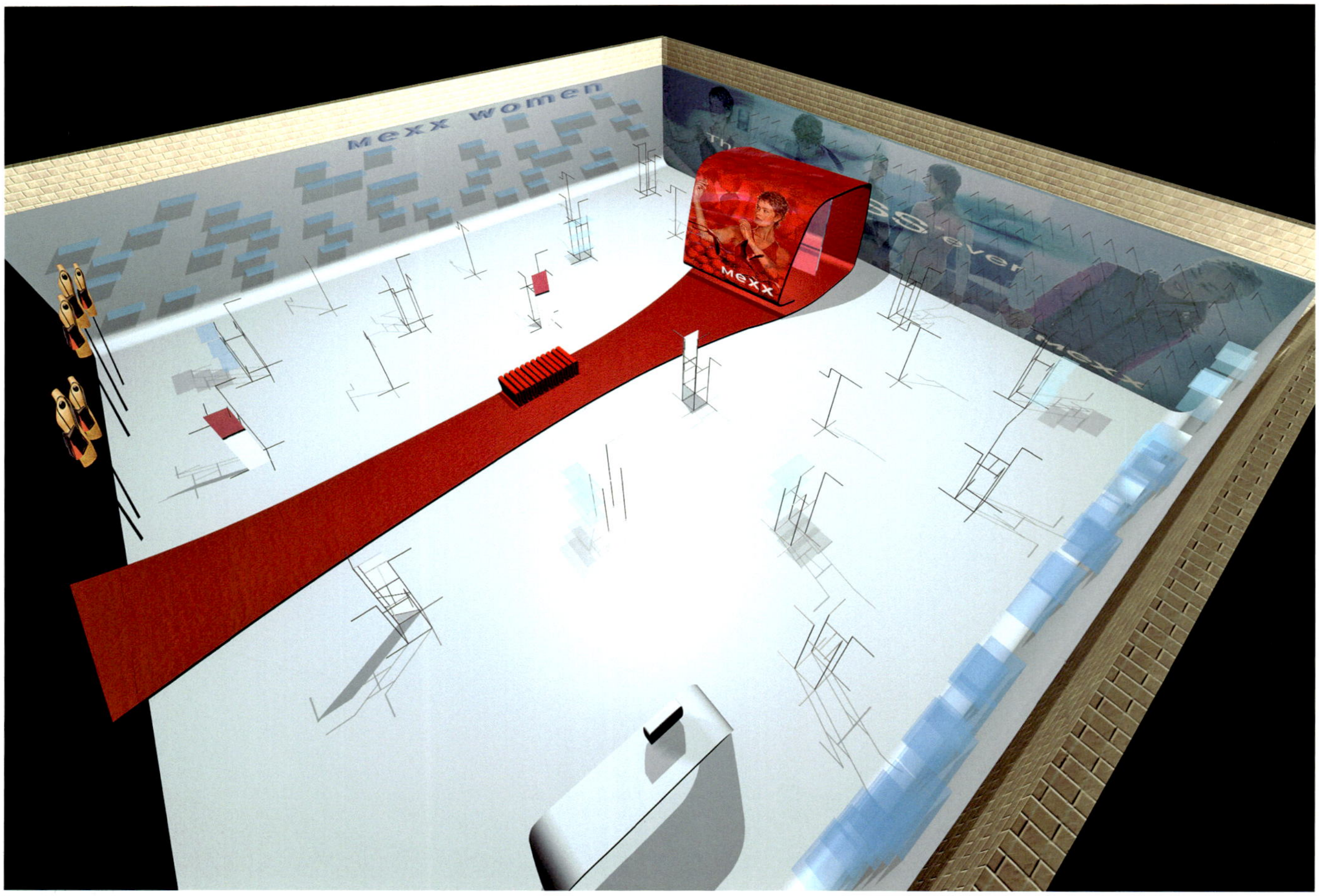

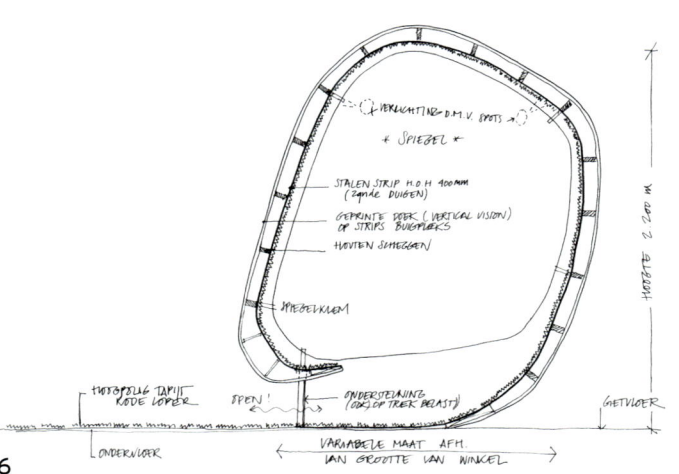

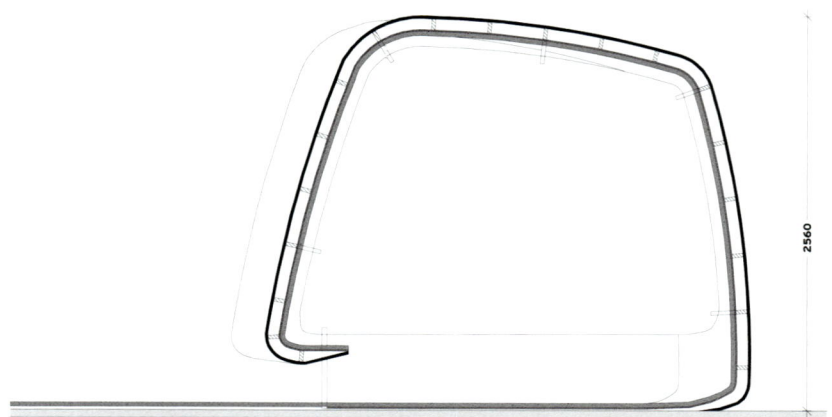

7

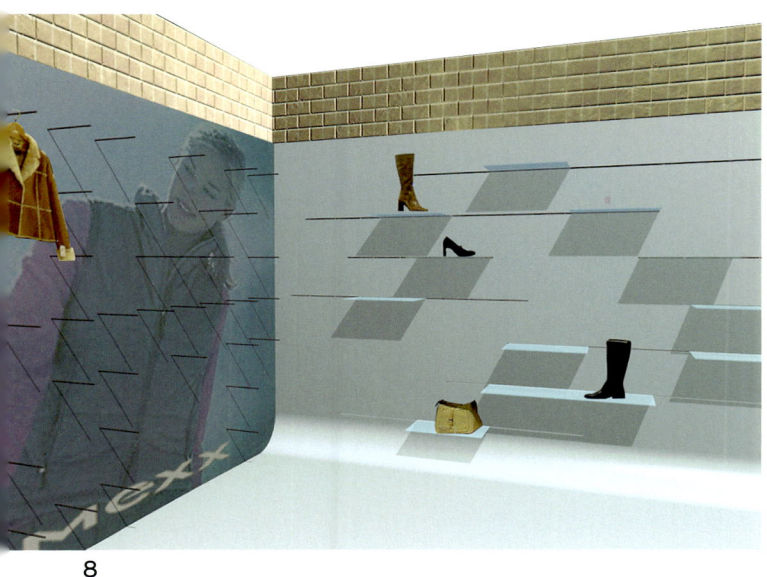

5 Rendering
6 Detail of dressing room
7 Section through dressing room
8 Detail of branding
9 Detail of red carpet

8

9

CLIENT: Ashlee House, London, England
DESIGN TEAM: Boris Zeisser, Maartje Lammers with Gerben Vos, Olav Bruin, Sabrina Kers
DESIGN: 2002–2003
CONSTRUCTION: 2003
FLOOR AREA: 200 square metres
BUILDING COSTS: €22,000

Ashlee House Hostel

LONDON, ENGLAND

A new interior was required for the reception area and lounge of the low-budget hostel Ashlee House in the centre of London. The result is a sophisticated space that merges past, present and future in an interior that's contemporary and edgy but still classic and timeless in style.

In the reception area, the former wall of the storage room and the office are now hidden behind a clever new curved wall that conceals any of the old uneven surfaces. On this curvaceous façade is a covering of custom-made wallpaper that features whimsical images pertaining to tourist icons and information, such as a map of the Underground and images of foggy London. The lampposts depicted on this wallpaper actually light up, giving the space a warm glow: a surreal view from the outsight at night.

For the lobby of the hostel an individual couch was custom designed, which further adds to the character and personality of the hostel.

In the lounge, situated in an unused room in the basement, a cosy space has been made thanks to more customised wallpaper featuring famous tourist attractions of London and its surroundings. By combining this wallpaper with a red floor and big leather seats and ashtrays, a new smoking room has been created: a welcome home away from home for the hostel's temporary inhabitants. ∎

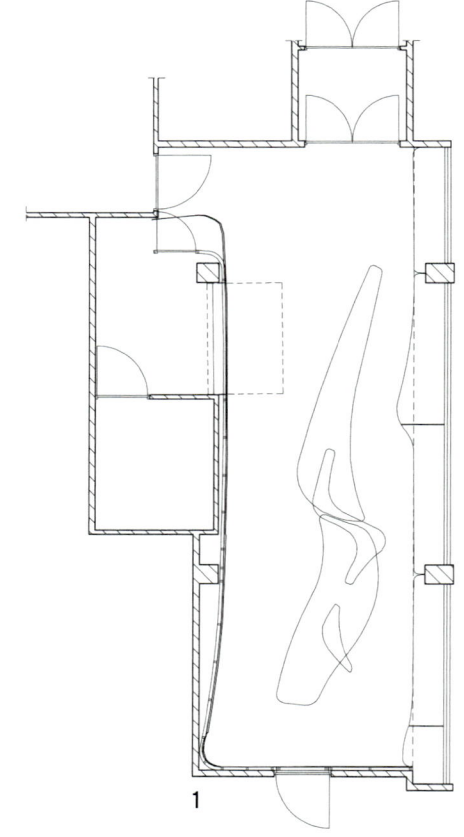

1

1 Reception area floor plan
2 Lobby seen from the street
Opposite Reception showing closed door

2

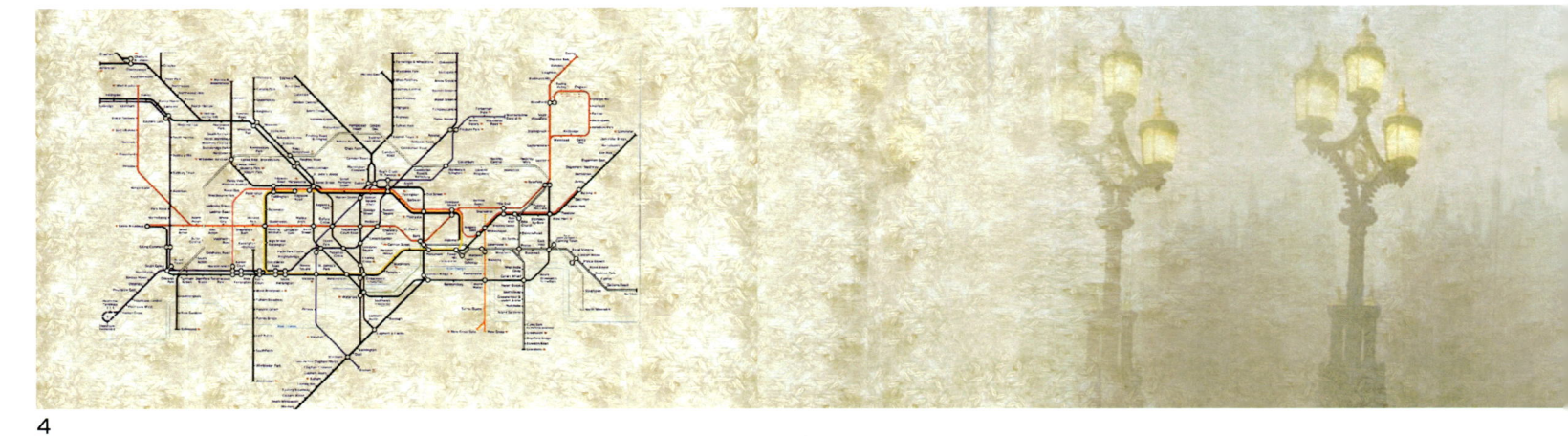

4

5

4 Custom-designed wallpaper
5 Backrest made of sheepskin
6 Detail of leather sofa
7 Details of lounge
8 Reception area with Underground wallpaper

6

7

8

CLIENT: Ymere, The Netherlands
DESIGN TEAM: Boris Zeisser, Maartje Lammers with Gerben Vos, Sabrina Kers, Fieke Poelman, Wouter Homs, Olav Bruin, Nora Rittmüller, Sylvain Grasset, Casper de Heer, Christian Schultze
DESIGN: 2003–2004
CONSTRUCTION: 2005–2006
FLOOR AREA: 7000 square metres
BUILDING COSTS: €5.2 million

Floriande Island 7 Housing

HOOFDDORP, THE NETHERLANDS

24H built 35 apartments and 34 family houses for social housing on the seventh of the Floriande Islands. This housing area is part of an urban plan for the 'Vinex' area in the town of Hoofddorp.

The two proposed apartment blocks are located on the north and south side, almost facing each other across the main public square, the 'Brink'. Next to the apartment blocks two-storey family houses are planned with a small private space on the Brink and private gardens at the back.

Hidden behind the northern buildings is a residential area called 'Park-Houses' with single-family social housing featuring large private gardens along narrow streets.

The façades of the houses are made from basalt combined with an aluminium plating. The façade cladding is given a horizontal and vertical accent by these materials. The slate basalt is used with rough and smooth reliefs. The gold-coloured anodised aluminium panels are, depending on what function they fulfill, either perforated or bubbled in a plane tree leaf pattern. ■

1

1 *Rendering of concept*
2 *Front façade of 'Park-Houses'*

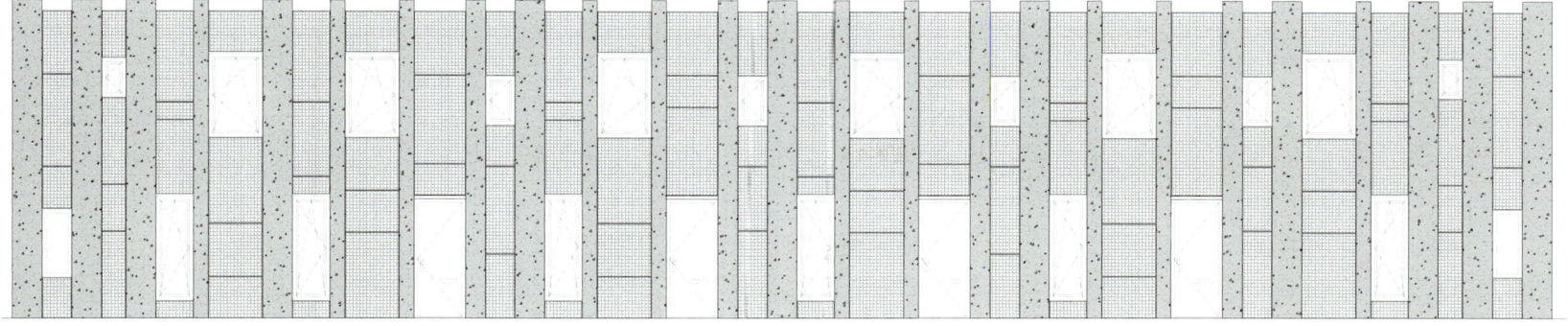

2

3 *Front façade south block*
4 *Detail of panels*
5 *Ground floor plan*
6 *Typical apartment floor plan*
7 *Stairs to level*

3

4

5

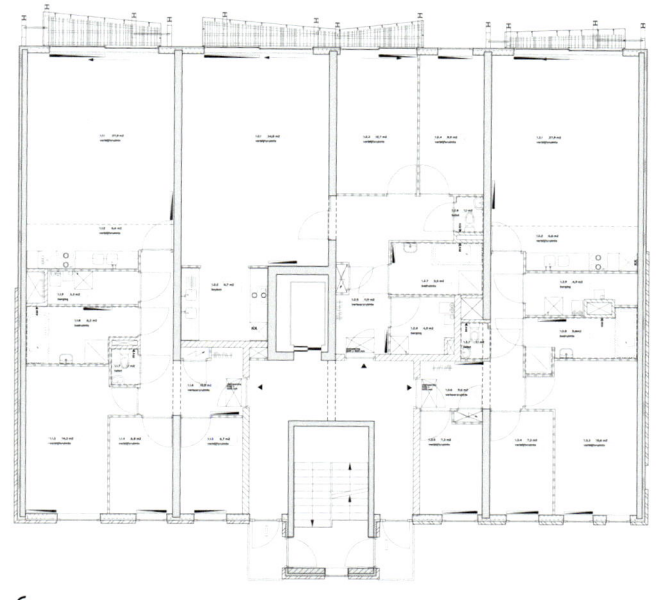

6

7

8 *Side façade of north block*
9 *Walkway*
10 *Floor plans of north block*

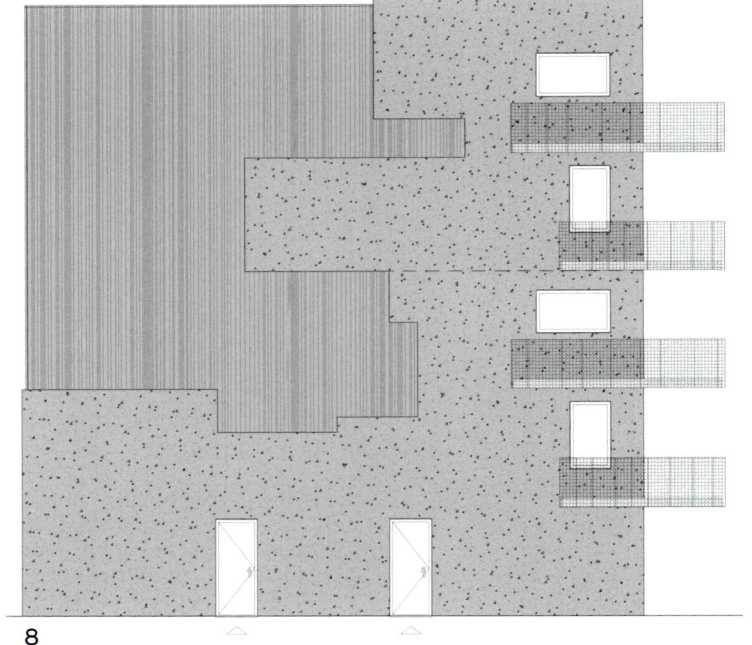

8

9

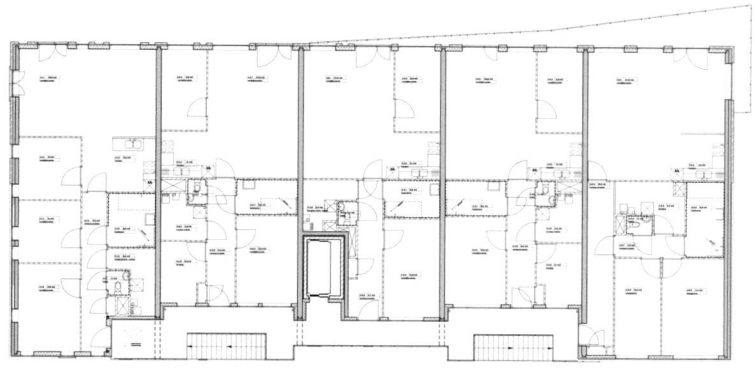

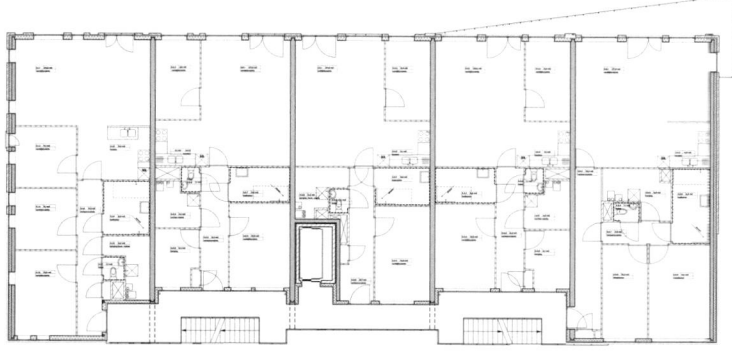

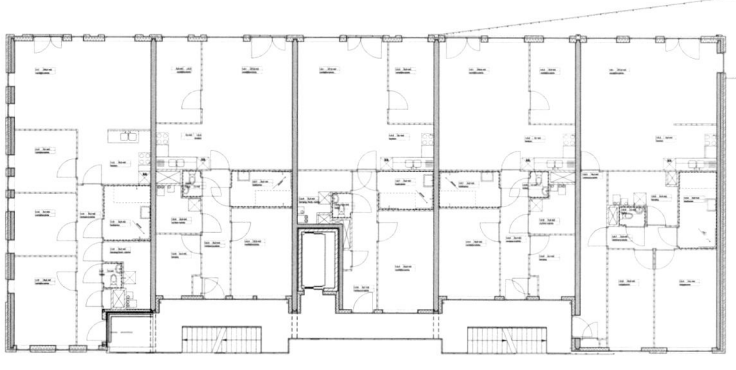

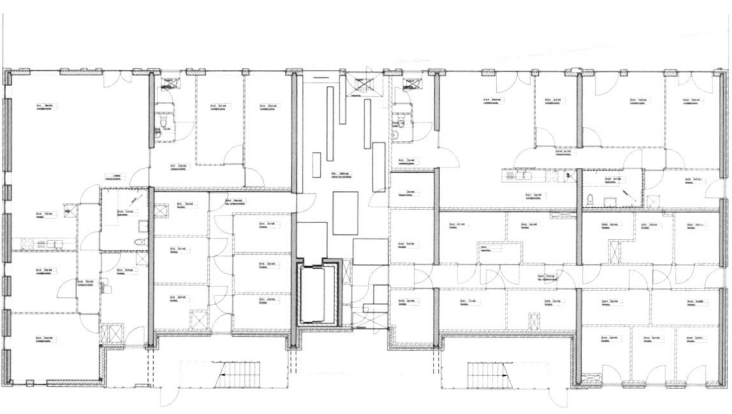

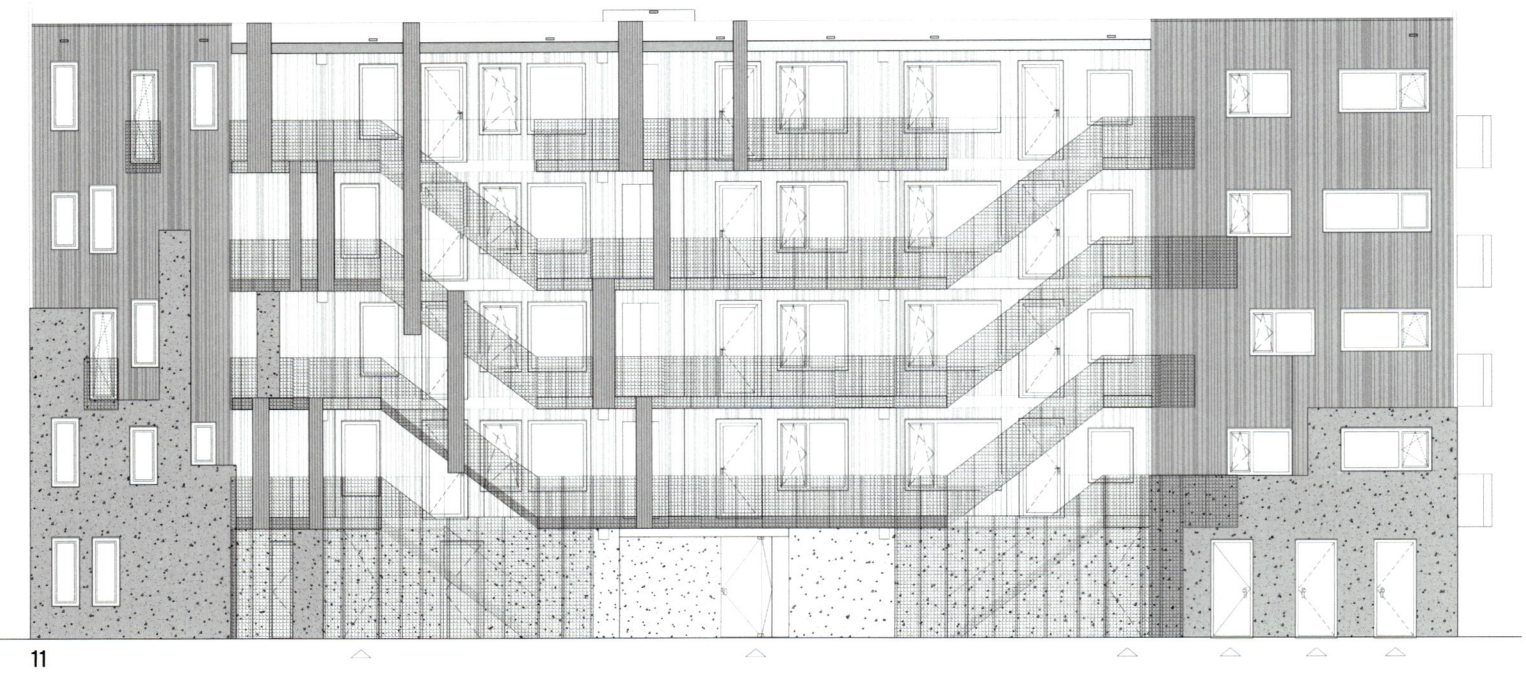

11

11   *Rear façade of north block*
12   *Detail of aluminium panels*
13   *Front façade of north block*
14   *Park Houses entrances*

12

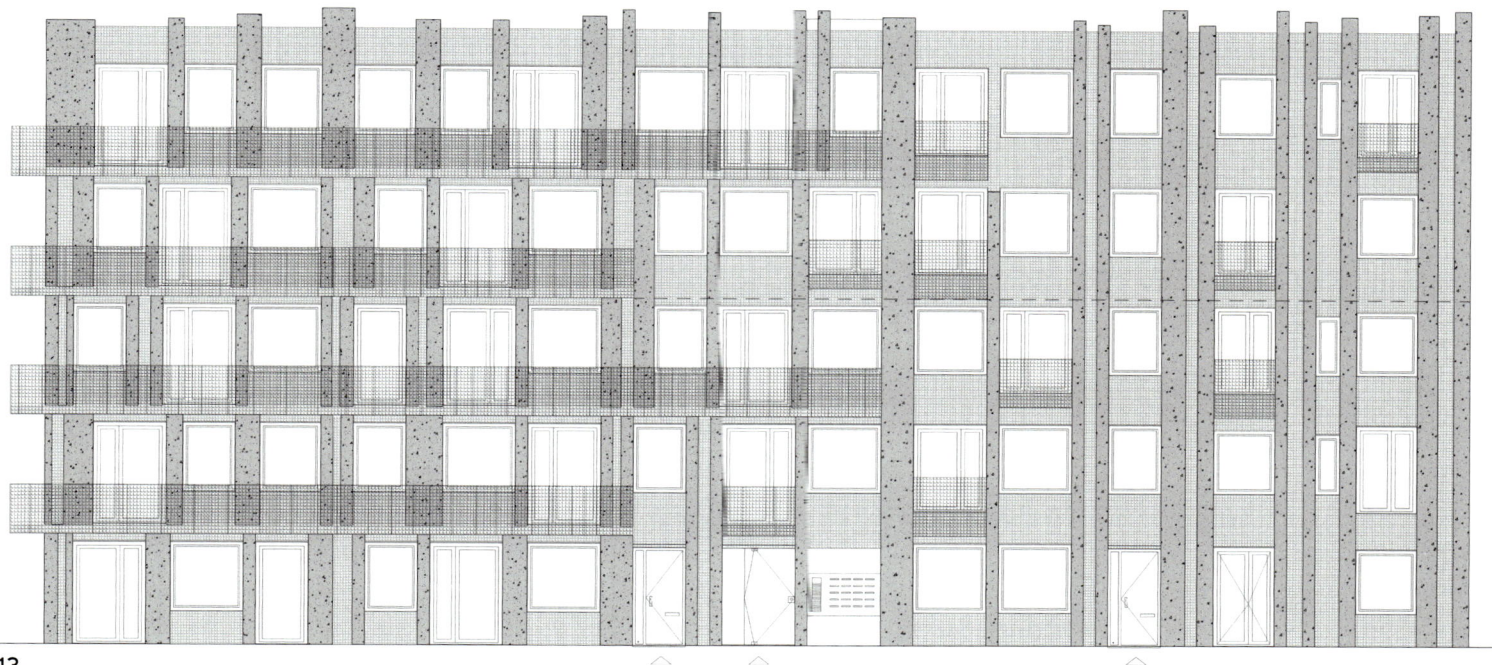

13

14

CLIENT: Municipality of Haarlem, Johan Matser Project Development, The Netherlands
DESIGN TEAM: Boris Zeisser, Maartje Lammers with Penney Nourney, Wouter Homs, Olav Bruin
DESIGN: 2004 (competition)
FLOOR AREA: 1200 square metres
BUILDING COSTS: €1.5 million

Schoterburcht Housing

HAARLEM, THE NETHERLANDS

Part of the philosophy developed for Schoterburcht Park by Haarlem's famous landscape architect Zochers is a mandate that dictates the park be rejuvenated and transformed into a city park based on the original values. The idea is for a true public space to be created for the inhabitants of Haarlem – a green oasis that is also easily accessible and visible.

The proposal is based on two main principles: to meet the objectives of the municipality and to develop a typology of housing that is characteristic of this specific and rare location.

Guided by the principles of a treehouse, with a small footprint and usable space in the crown of the tree, three contemporary sculptures were developed.

The sculptures were placed at strategic positions on the site, thus optimising the historical axis and the existing sightlines.

Further design of the sculptures resulted in sturdy characters: named rhinoceros, buffalo and heron. From their various roofscapes they react to the existing monumental complex, making a worthy addition to the 21st century; a monument for the future. ■

1

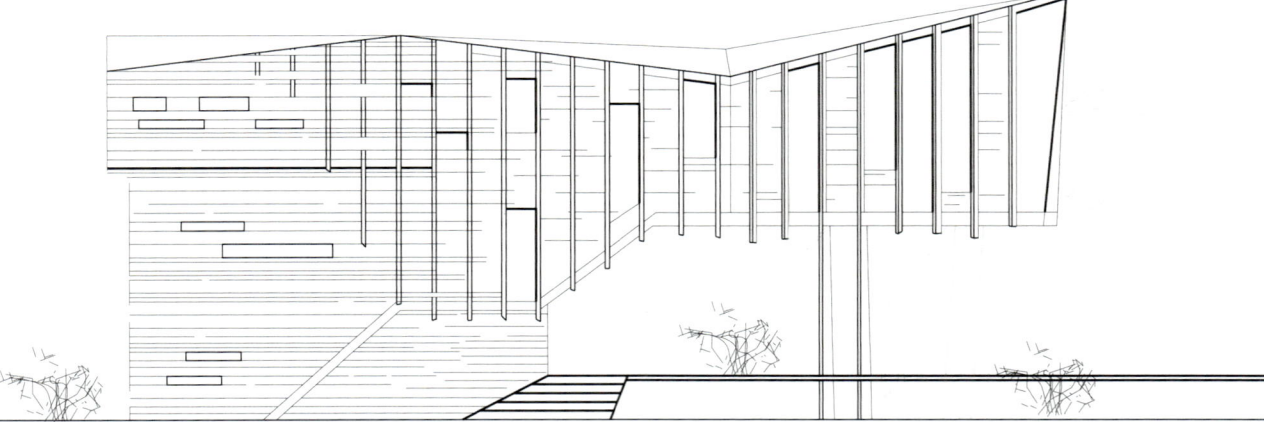

2

1 *View from Kleverpark area*
2 *Façade of 'Rhinoceros'*
3 *Detail of private terrace in public space*
4 *Rendering of 'Rhinoceros'*

5

5 *'Buffalo' seen from park*
6 *Site plan*
7 *Plans of 'Heron'*

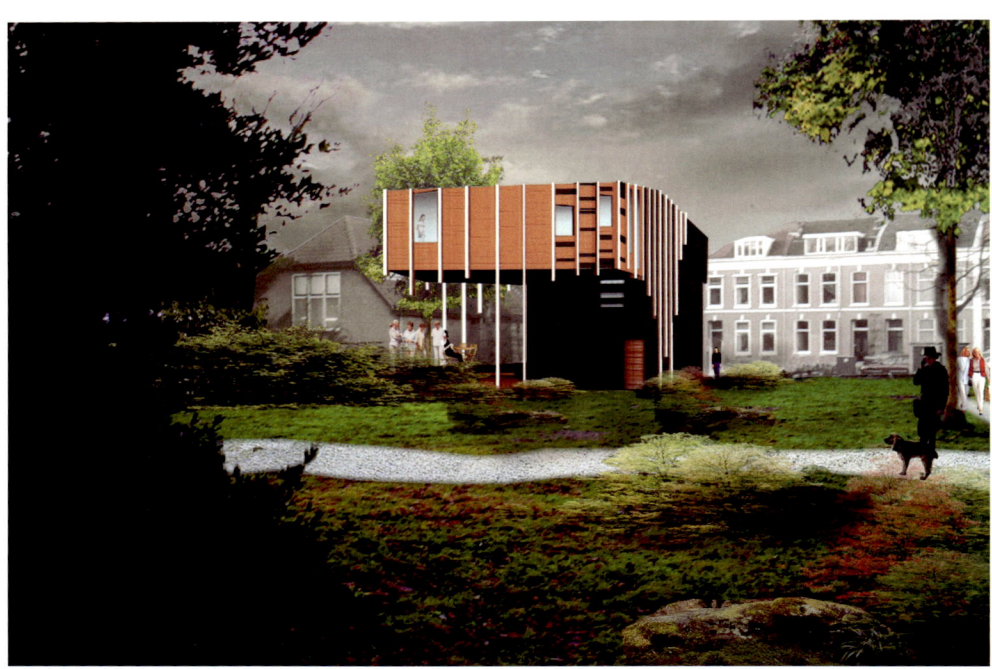

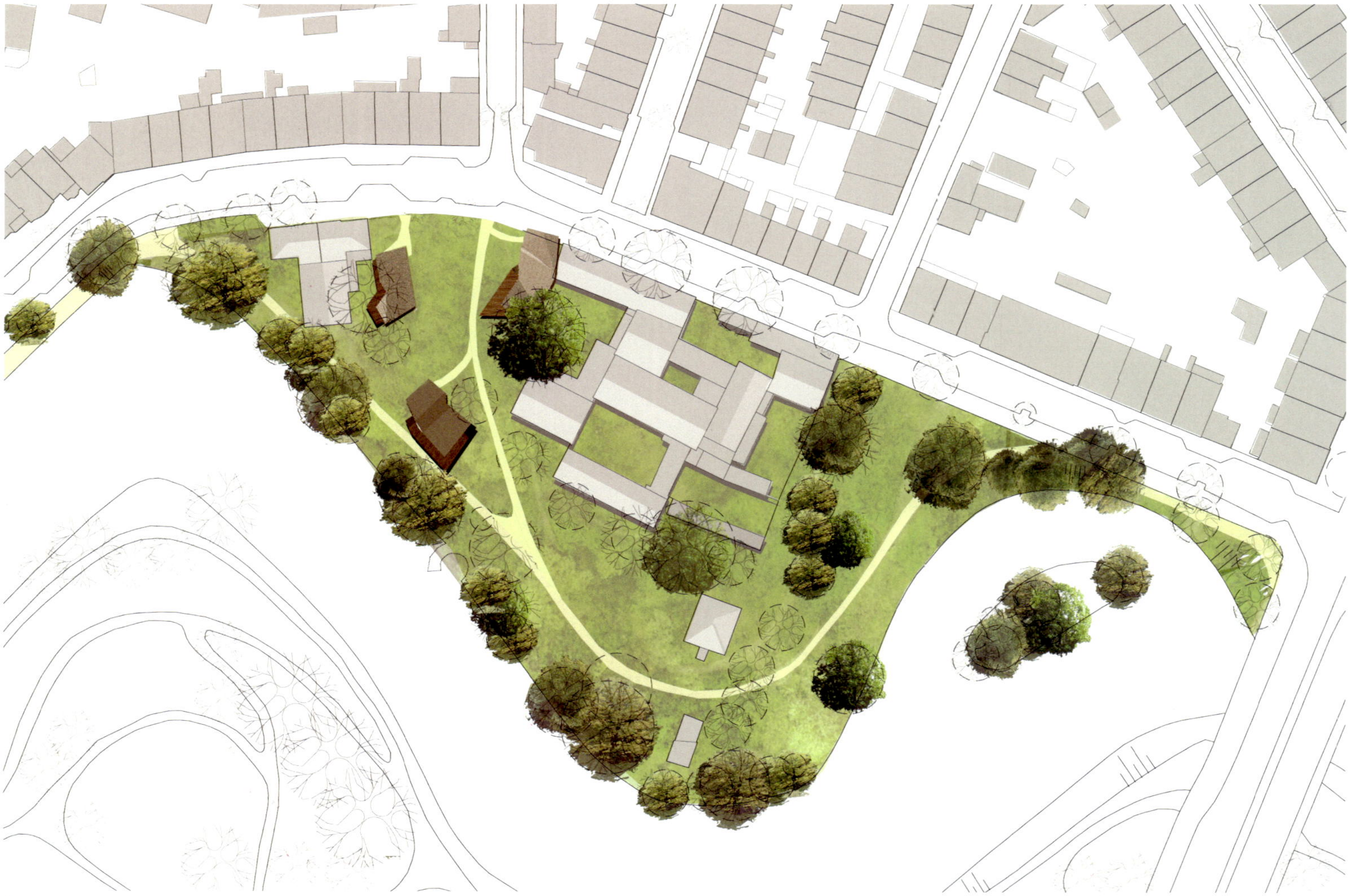

6

7

8

9

10

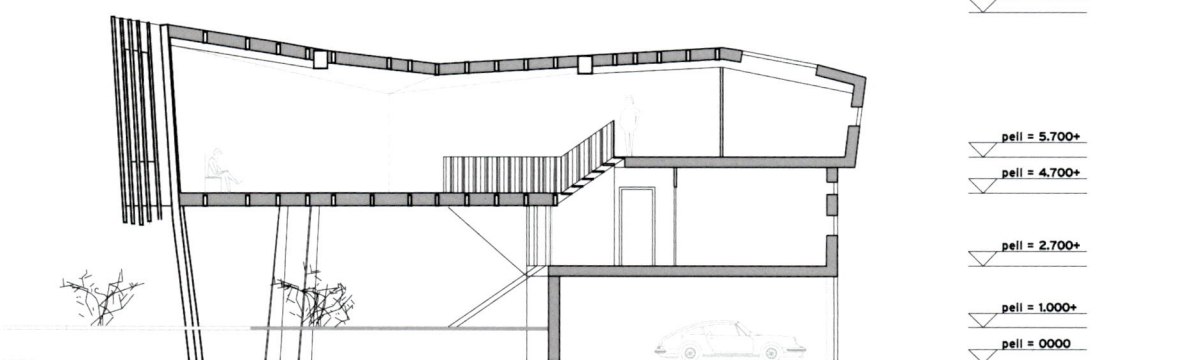

peil = 9.700+

peil = 5.700+

peil = 4.700+

peil = 2.700+

peil = 1.000+

peil = 0000

11

12

14

15

16

8–10, 14–16   *Various views of model*
          11   *Section of 'Rhinoceros'*
          12   *Aerial view of model*
          13   *Floor plans of 'Rhinoceros'*

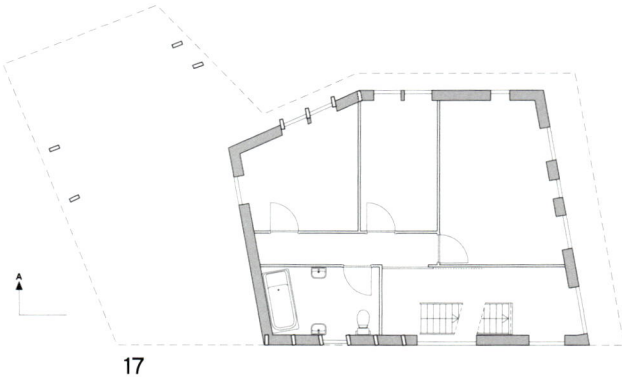

17

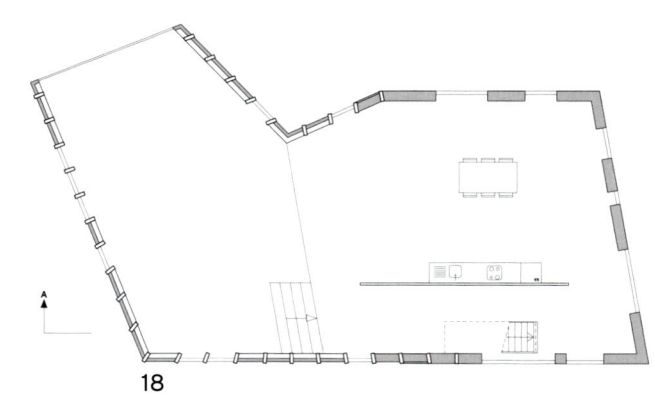

18

60

19

20

21

17 *Top floor plan of 'Buffalo'*
18 *Living room plan of 'Buffalo'*
19–21, 23–25 *Model detail views*
22 *Ground floor plan of 'Buffalo'*

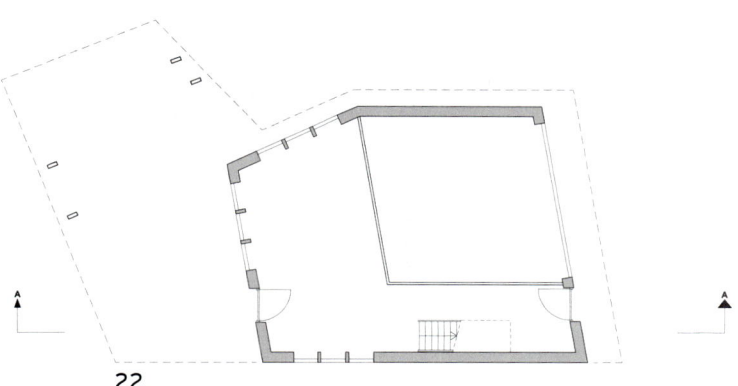

22

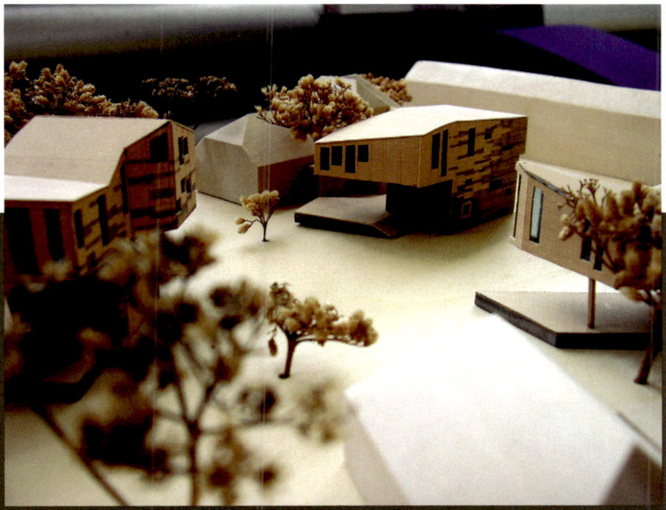

23

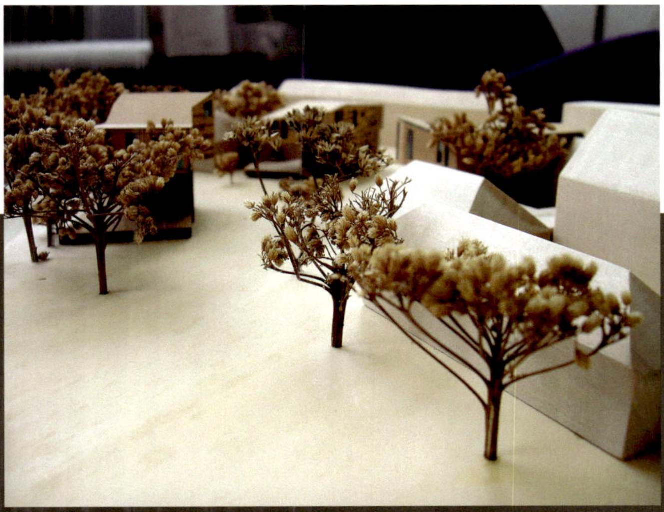

24

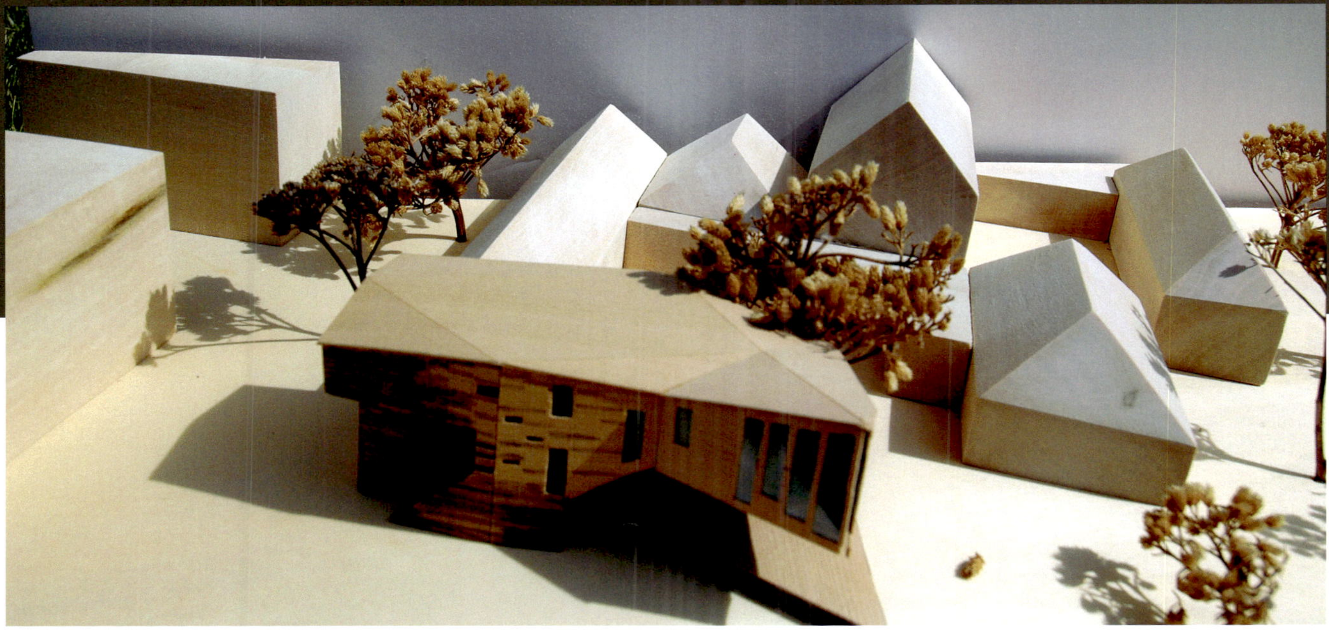

25

CLIENT: Heddes Vastgoed, Hoorn, The Netherlands
DESIGN TEAM: Boris Zeisser, Maartje Lammers with Fieke Poelman, Sabrina Kers, Sandor Marks, Jacopo van der Horst, Sabine Simon, Nora Rittmüller, Marie Allard-Latour, Saman Saffarian, Ben de Lange, Arnout Verweij, Susan Hoekstra, Olav Bruin, Sarah van Apeldoorn
DESIGN: 2003–2006
CONSTRUCTION: 2006–2007
FLOOR AREA: 14,000 square metres
BUILDING COSTS: €14 million

Sciencepark Housing

AMSTERDAM, THE NETHERLANDS

Within the urban scheme of the Kees Christiaanse-designed Sciencepark in Amsterdam, 24H was commissioned to come up with a proposal for one of the five housing projects, called 'The Twins'. The location is between the Oosterringdijk Dike and the Caroline Mac Gillavrylaan.

24H's proposal for the two apartment blocks, which will be 17 and 14 storeys high, is to create a sensitive urban environment encompassing 87 dwellings. Within this design, two L-shaped volumes will slide under each other and be connected through a plinth containing housing and parking. The smaller west tower will sit flush with the east one, opening up views and creating an entrance from the dike and the street, as well as access to parking. The east tower will stand on the ground and allow direct access to the houses on street level: its main entrance and lobby establishing a visual connection between the dike and the Caroline Mac Gillavrylaan, with vertical circulation in the centre.

The façade is made up of a fine grid of slate and glass. Variations in colour from brown to grey, as the towers rise, connect the building to the elements: brown at the bottom, where the towers rise up from the ground; and grey towards the top giving the impression of fading away into the air.

The skin tapers outwards at specific parts of the towers to create a noise barrier from the nearby railway. ■

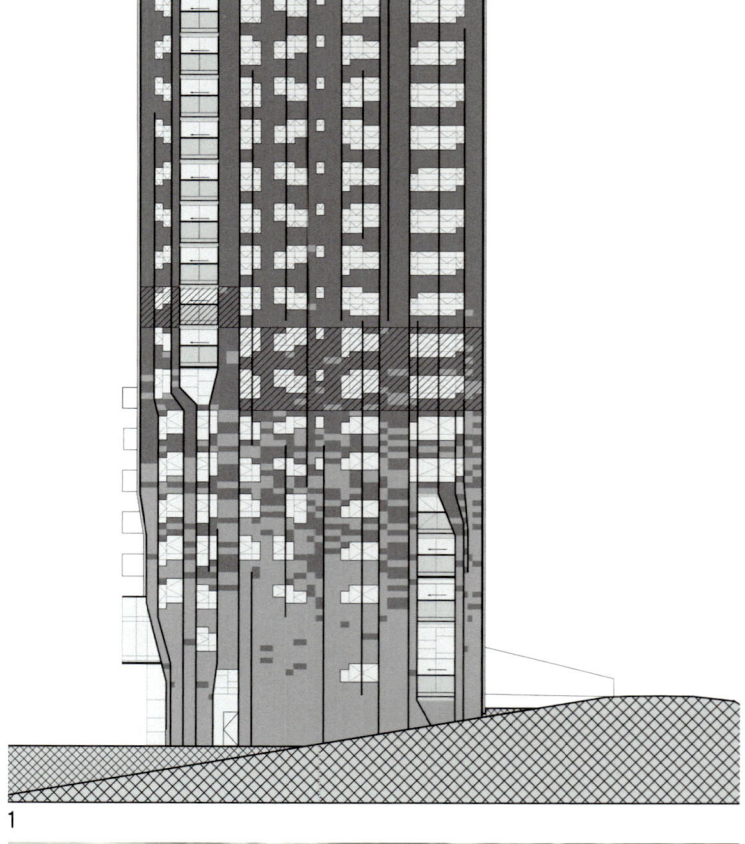

1

2

1 Elevation of east tower
2 View from west along the dike
3 View from Caroline Mac Gillavrylaan
4 View from west along the dike
5 View from Valentynkade
6 North elevation

3

4

5

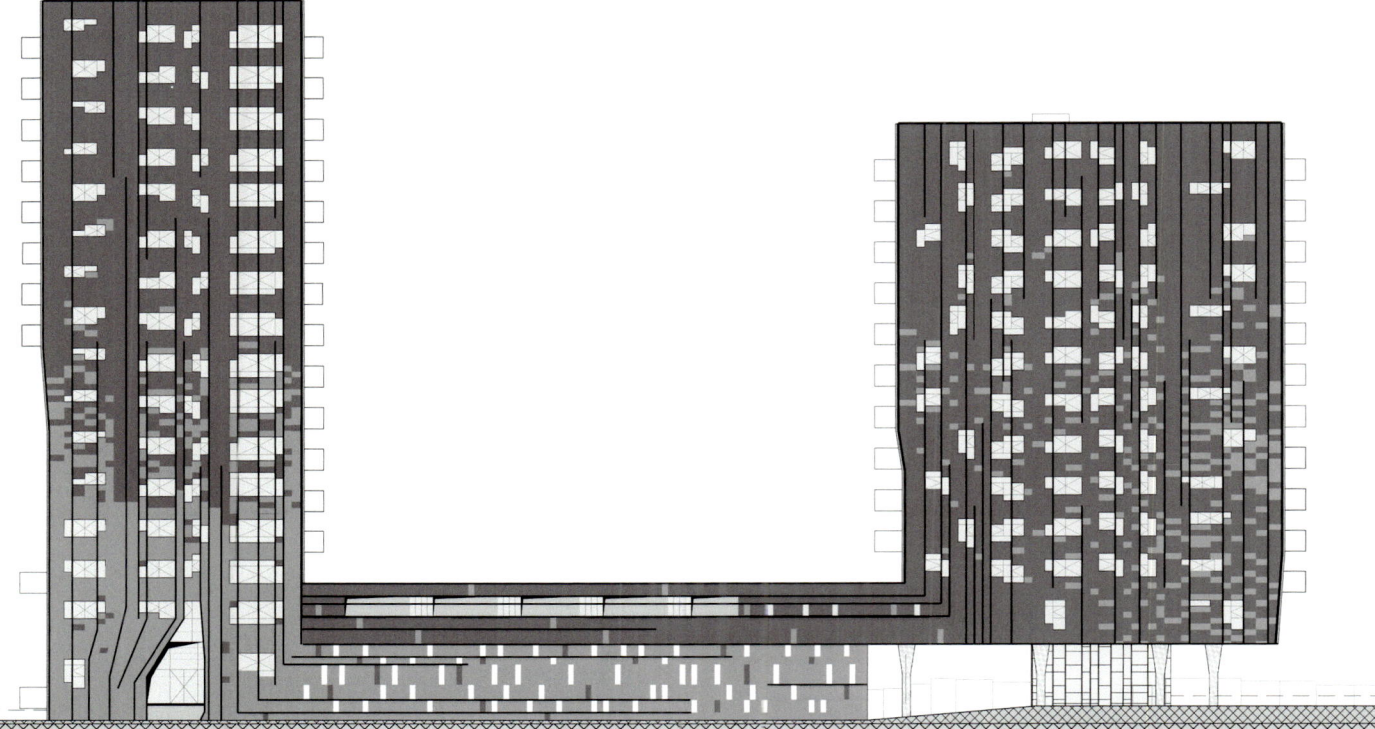

6

CLIENT: Aco Mode Agentur, Vienna, Austria
DESIGN TEAM: Boris Zeisser, Maartje Lammers with Ruben Bergambagt, Michele Stramezzi, Sylvain Grasset
DESIGN: 2004–2005
FLOOR AREA: 900 square metres
BUILDING COSTS: €300,000

Fashion Cave
SALZBURG, AUSTRIA

Hidden behind a showroom of the Aco Fashion Agentur in Salzburg lie a couple of caves, dug by Russian prisoners of war during the Second World War to protect the population of Salzburg. Now in use as storage space, the idea was to transform these natural theatrical spaces into a showroom during the fashion season and, during the off-season, a multi-functional space for parties and events.

The present expression of the entrance and the underlying course to these caves do not fit the new functions at all. There are also two identical caves that will ultimately fulfill two different functions. The challenge was in creating a design that not only made the most of these dramatic spaces and gave them an extra layer of theatre, but successfully turned them into productive spaces for work or play.

The most imaginative solution was to design a moving entrance curtain, which then led visitors through a 'walk of fame' gallery to the first parabolic party space, and finally a baroque ballroom. In addition, the design includes a high floor, complete with a glass strip, that functions as catwalk but at the same time reveals the historic cave and its natural textured surfaces underneath.

The first step is to build a party space, with materials that are suitably glamorous. The walls are to be constructed of transparent glass and timber panelling, which allows the mood to develop from the inside out. To enhance the design, the walls of the cave are to be visible through the glass panels, and highlighted by integrated lighting.

It is envisaged the final space will be both eclectic and exciting, creating a dramatic and stylish backdrop for any soirée, big or small. ■

1

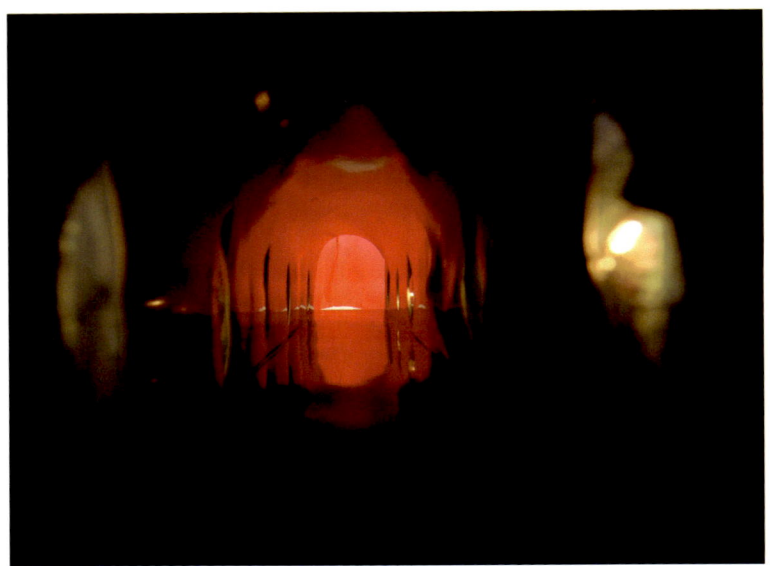

2

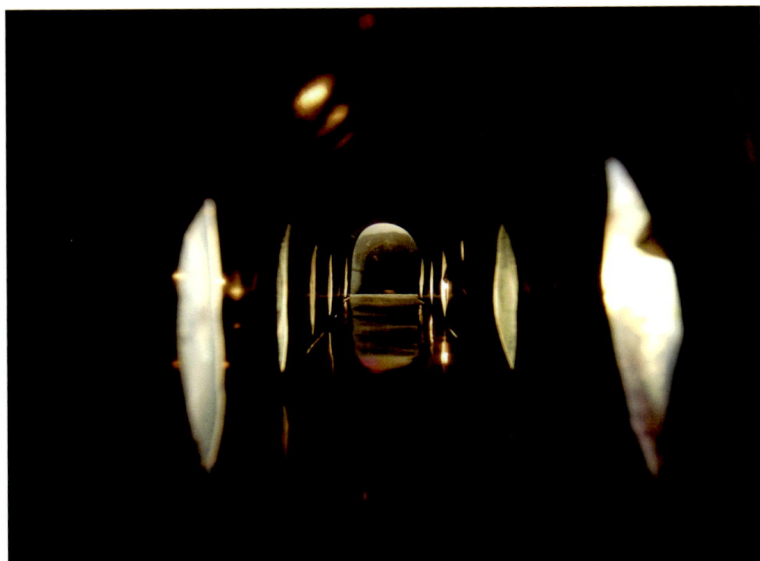

3

2&3 *Impressions of sculpture gallery*
  4 *Floor plan of fashion cave*
  5 *Diagram showing wall connection to floor*
  6 *Section of raised glass floor*
  7 *Evening fashion show*

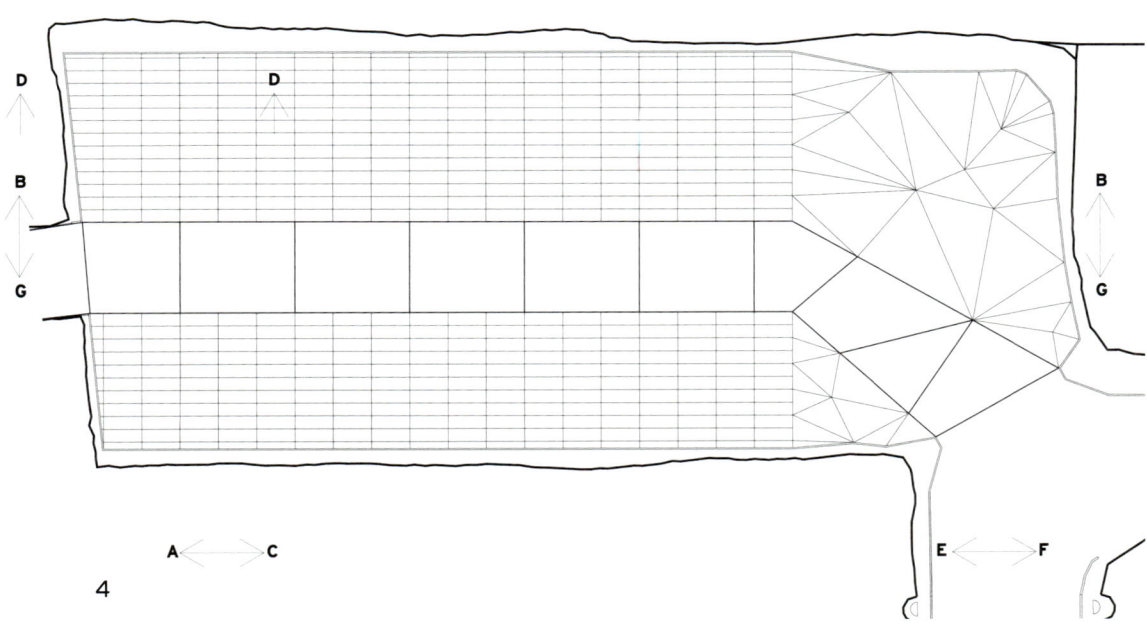

4

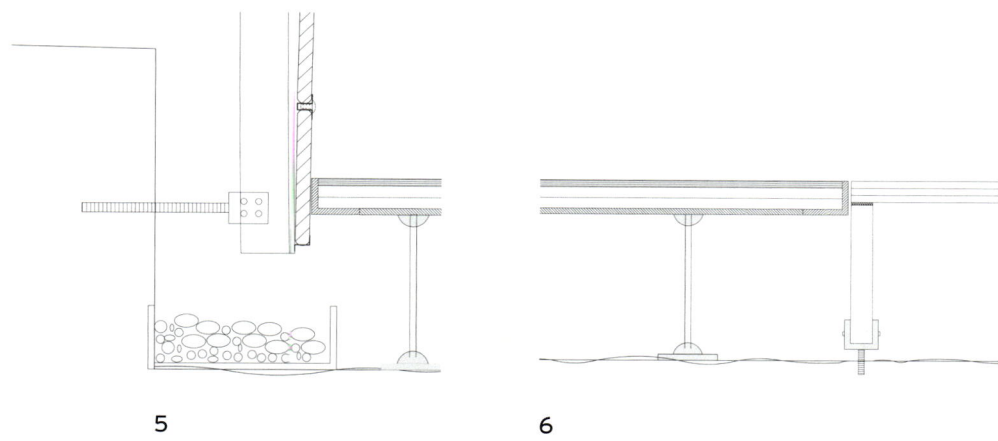

5

6

7

CLIENT: Municipality of Peckham/Camberwell Arts College, London, England
DESIGN TEAM: Boris Zeisser, Maartje Lammers with Ruben Bergambagt, Marie Allard Latour
DESIGN: 2005 (competition)
FLOOR AREA: 150 square metres
BUILDING COSTS: €350,000

Arts Pavilion

PECKHAM, LONDON, ENGLAND

When it came to designing the Arts Pavilion in Peckham, London, there were aspects of the location that were important considerations. These included the location itself, the position in front of Will Alsops' library, as well as the social aspects of the location. During the day the building had to have maximum accessibility; at night it had to be possible to secure it.

The design was based on a 'sculpture', comprising smaller, independent buildings that could be transported to other locations if necessary and reconfigured to create new spaces. Within Peckham Square the elements of the sculpture could be moved, via a rail in the footpath, and repositioned in such a way that during opening hours the functions of the building would become visible. At the same time, the new public routes over the square, past the café, bookshop and reception, would become more accessible and also more visible.

By opening up this 'sculpture' into its different elements the existing pockets of dead space are therefore dissolved, and become lively and vibrant parts of the public space. The building also interacts with the daily use of the square with this flexible design.

As well, through its mysterious architectural character, the sculpture challenges and invites people to investigate it further. Both physically and spiritually the sculpture and its transparent content form a threshold over which people can step and explore another creative world, while at the same time being inspired to shape and plan their own aspirations. The creative design quite literally helps people find a new route through the world of the arts. ∎

1

2

3

1 *Urban setting*
2&4 *Moving through the opened sculpture*
3 *Rendering of opened sculpture*

4

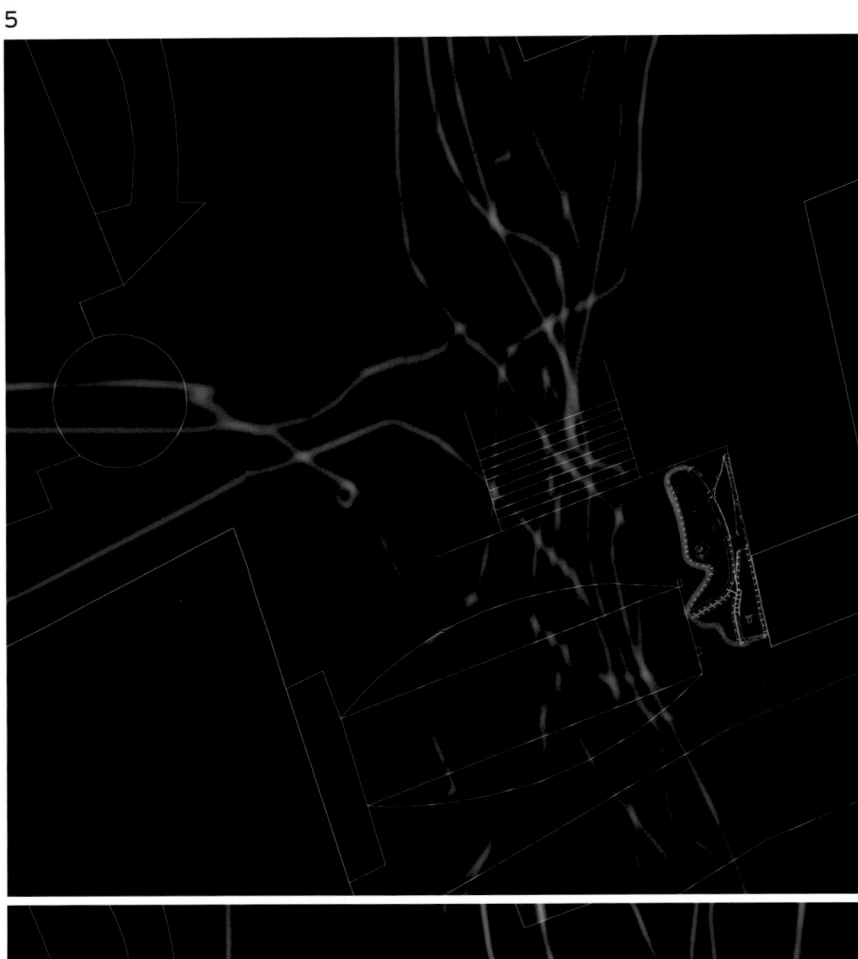

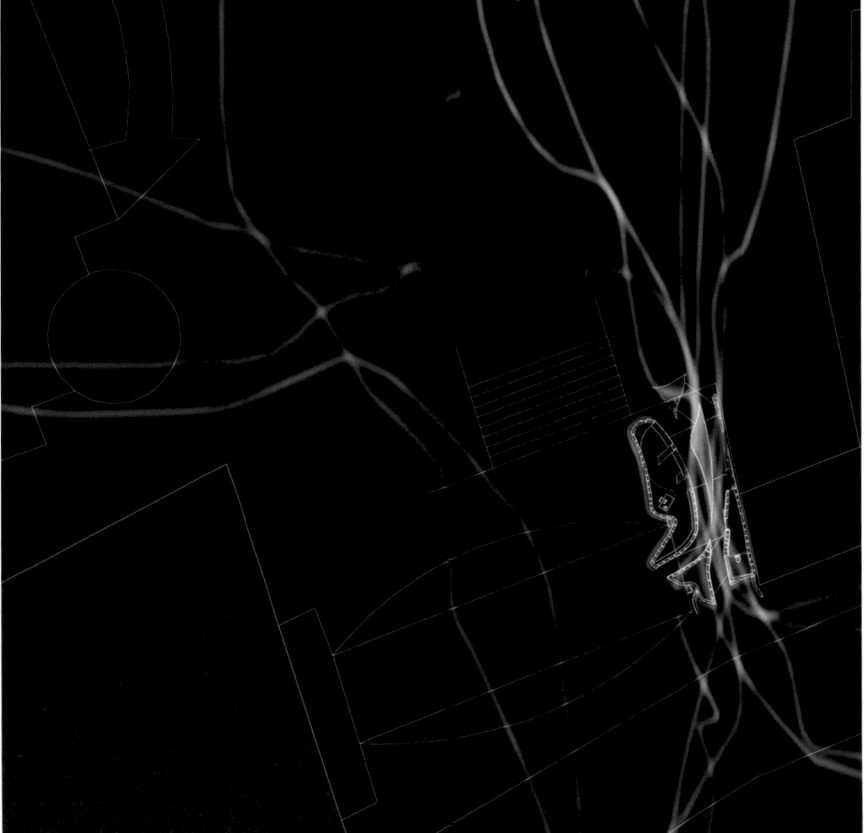

5 *Pedestrian routes at night*
6 *Pedestrian routes during the day*
7 *Sculpture closed at night*
8 *Sculpture opened at dusk*

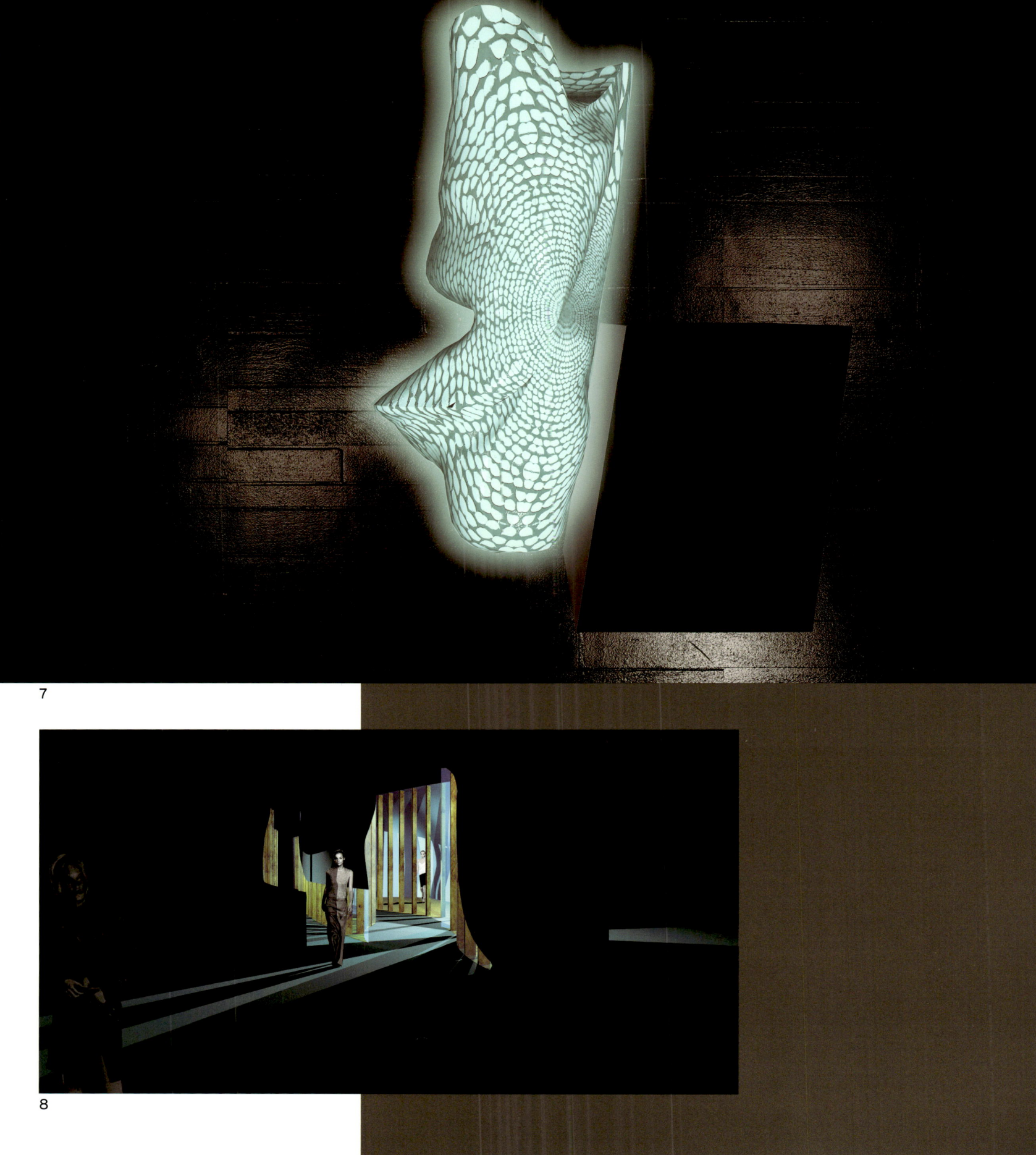

7

8

9

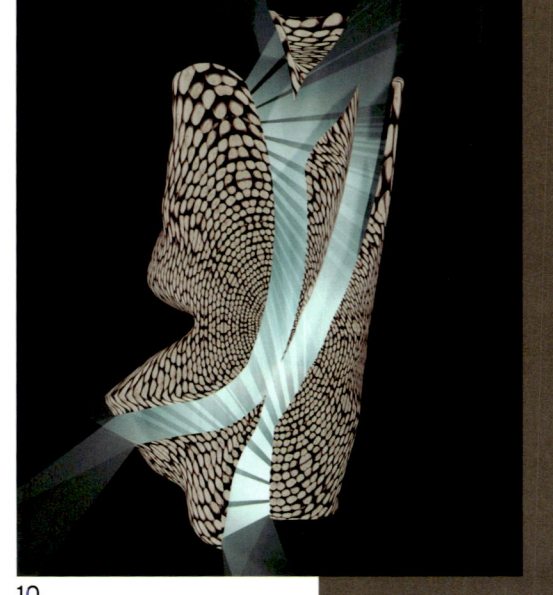

10

9 *Pavilion open during the day*
10 *Pavilion open at night*
11 *Pavilion closed*

11

CLIENT: Portaal, Amersfoort, The Netherlands
DESIGN TEAM: Boris Zeisser, Maartje Lammers with Saman Saffarian, Bruno Toledo
DESIGN: 2005
FLOOR AREA: 40,000 square metres
BUILDING COSTS: €36 million

Hybrid Housing Complex

SMITSVEEN PARK, SOEST, THE NETHERLANDS

24H is redeveloping a part of the Smitsveen Quarter in Soest. Four hundred new dwellings are planned for this development, including apartments as well as family houses.

The starting point for this design is to keep all existing green areas and most of the full-grown trees. The design concept will then take note of the spaces defined by the green areas and plan new housing accordingly.

The new district needs its own character, so the location is to be divided into three different neighbourhoods, each with their own personality.

One of them is the lively city street with various types of apartments and family houses. Access is provided via the front door on the streetscape, while at the back the emphasis is on an active relationship with the landscape.

Mainly low-rise buildings are planned for the second neighbourhood. A small amount of family houses will be put together underneath one roof and spread over the area. The residents can park on their own plot. Access to the houses is a winding road through the park.

A high-rise building will be created behind existing apartment blocks on the other side of the district. Services, required by community, are planned for the ground floor with parking underneath. The high-rise apartment block of the third neighbourhood acts as a landmark for the Smitsveen Park district and is easily recognisable from its surroundings. ■

1&2 *Renderings of landscape*

1

3

4

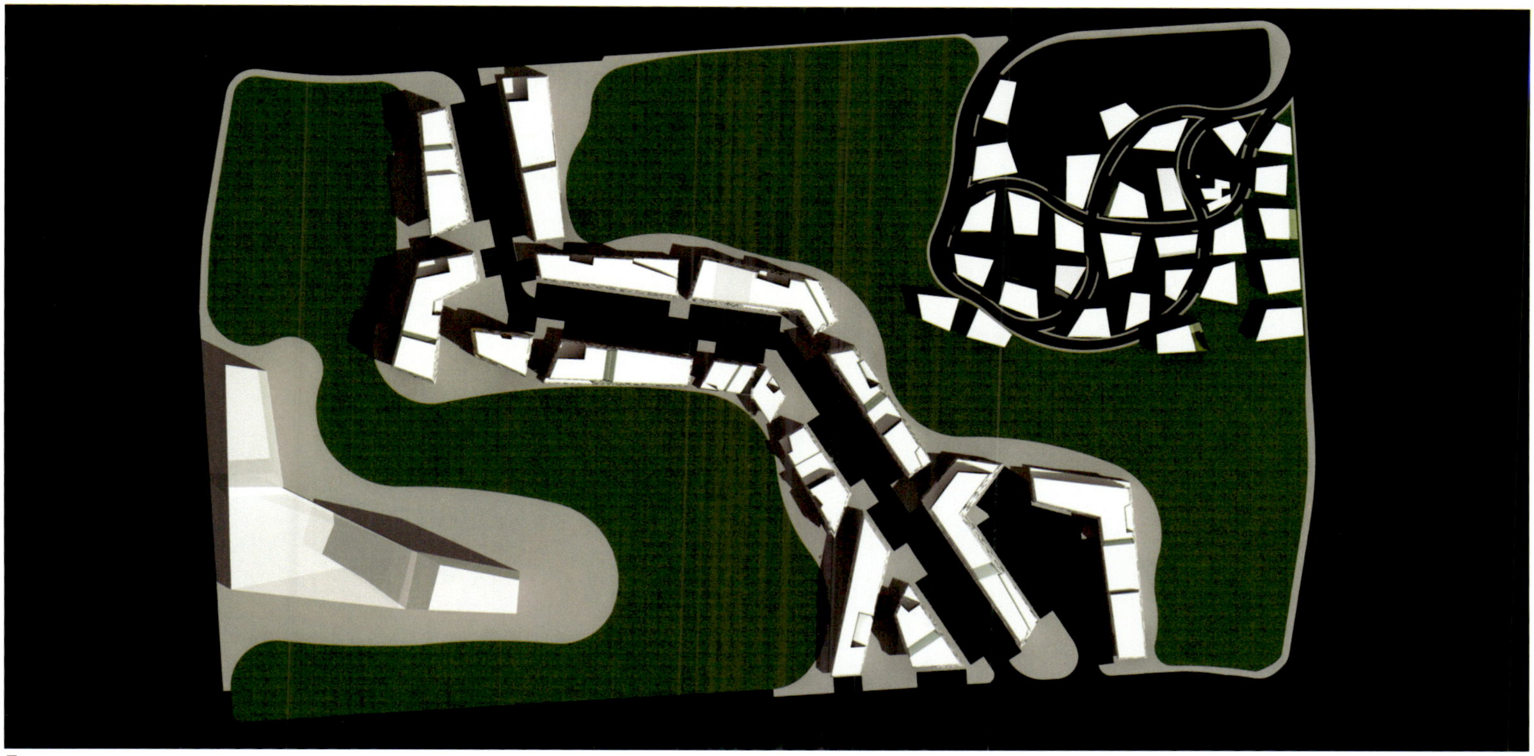

5

3&4 *Renderings of landscape*
  5 *Site plan*

GROEN DIAGRAM   BESTAAND GROEN
                GROEPEREN & INTERPRETATIE BESTAAND GROEN

6

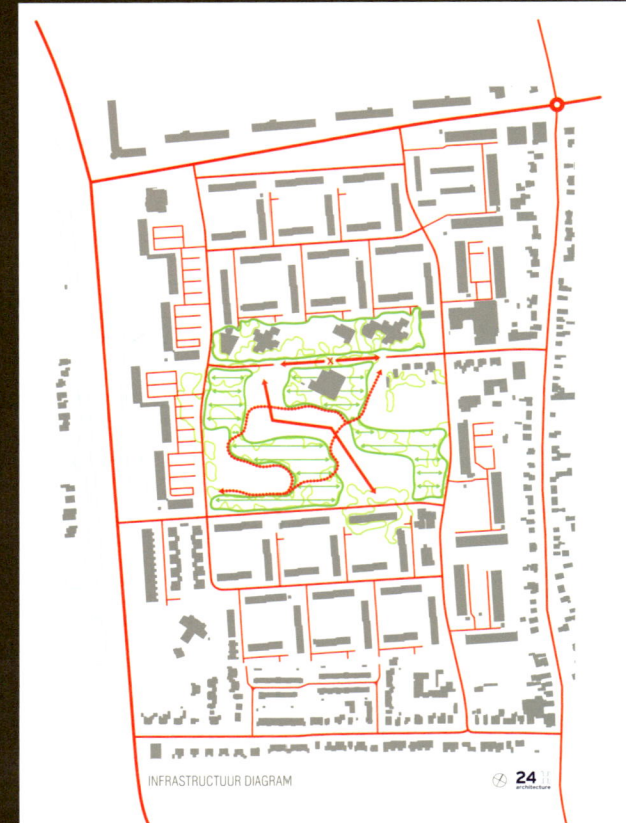

INFRASTRUCTUUR DIAGRAM

7

8

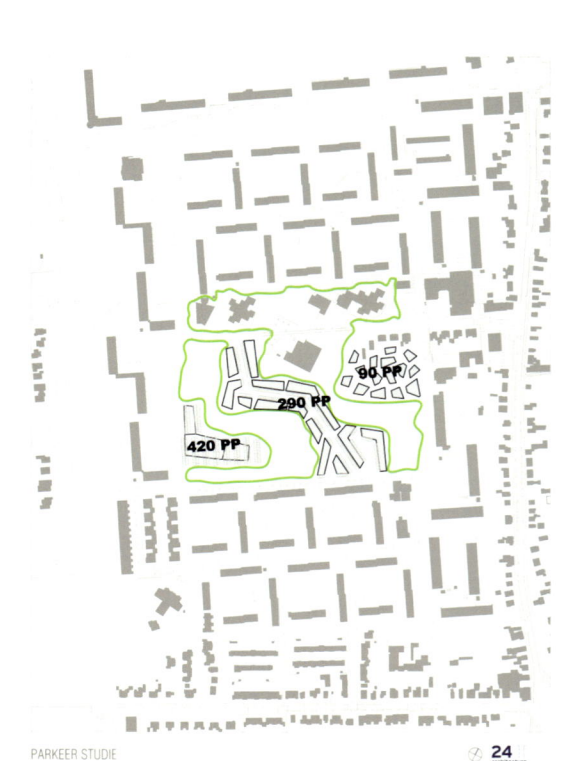

PARKEER STUDIE

9

10

11

12

6 *Analysis of landscape*
7 *Inventory of connecting routes*
8 *Number of dwellings*
9 *Total composition*
10–13 *Model views*

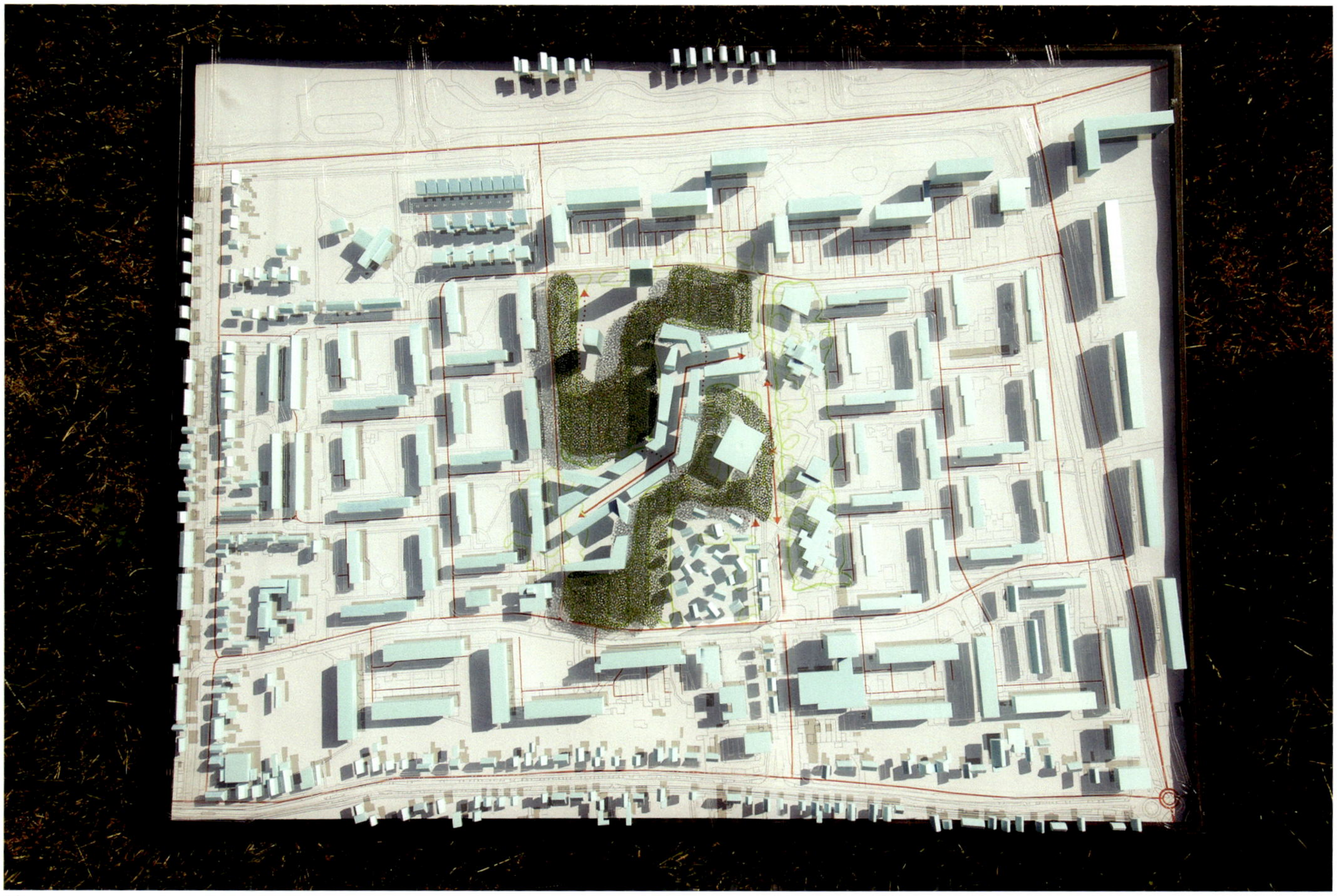

13

DICHTHEID DIAGRAM · 24 architecture

0 - 10	100 - 110	200 - 210
10 - 20	110 - 120	210 - 220
20 - 30	120 - 130	220 - 230
30 - 40	130 - 140	230 - 240
40 - 50	140 - 150	240 - 250
50 - 60	150 - 160	250 - 260
60 - 70	160 - 170	260 - 270
70 - 80	170 - 180	270 - 280
80 - 90	180 - 190	280 - 290
90 - 100	190 - 200	290 - 300

DICHTHEID DIAGRAM · 24 architecture

14

14   *Analysis of density of Smitsveen*
15   *Impression of central area*
16   *Analysis of density of Smitsveen*
17   *Site plan*

DICHTHEID DIAGRAM

TOTAAL OPPERVLAK SITE
AANTAL VERDIEPINGEN
TOTAAL OPPERVLAK BEGANE GROND GEBOUW
TOTAAL VLOER OPPERVLAK
TOTAAL GEBOUW VOLUME
GEBOUW HOOGTE
INWONERS

24 architecture

INFRASTRUCTUUR DIAGRAM

24 architecture

16   17

CLIENT: Kunsthal, Rotterdam, The Netherlands
DESIGN TEAM: Boris Zeisser, Maartje Lammers with Michele Stramezzi, Nora Rittmüler
DESIGN: 2005
CONSTRUCTION: 2005
FLOOR AREA: 2000 square metres

'Meesters van de Romantiek' Exhibition

KUNSTHAL, ROTTERDAM, THE NETHERLANDS

The 'Meesters van de Romantiek' exhibition was a collabaration between the Kunsthal in Rotterdam and the Rijksmuseum in Amsterdam. Ronald de Leeuw, director of the Rijksmuseum, worked as guest curator for almost five years on this project to showcase Dutch Romantic art. It was held within the Kunsthal's Rem Koolhaas building.

Within the Romantic Movement two extremes are visible: a narrow-minded view of the world and a love for freedom. This was visible in the Romantic paintings through neat portraits on one hand and expressions of degenerated nature on the other.

These extremes were an important source of inspiration for the exhibition's design, and resulted in the expression of a 'living room' with benches, chandeliers, floral wallpaper and pictures on the walls at one end and a sculptural rock, tree-trunks and branches as banisters at the other. The enormous walls were sealed with coloured Lycra, concealing natural elements such as deer antlers, stuffed birds, shells and pineapples, all of which emerged from underneath the walls. Most of these elements were, naturally, placed at the wildlife side of the exhibition. The exhibition then 'grew' from nature to the 'living room', with four sub-themes bridging the two extremes. Thus the space developed from the rigid orthogonality of the man-made living room to the wild expressiveness of walls at the wildlife side.

Providing a 'missing link' in the design was a set of stairs that created a connection to Hall 3 of the Kunsthal, which was also set up with oil paintings and drawings by Romantic artists. ■

1 *Sightline through exhibition*
2 *Section through stairs*
3 *View through gallery*

1

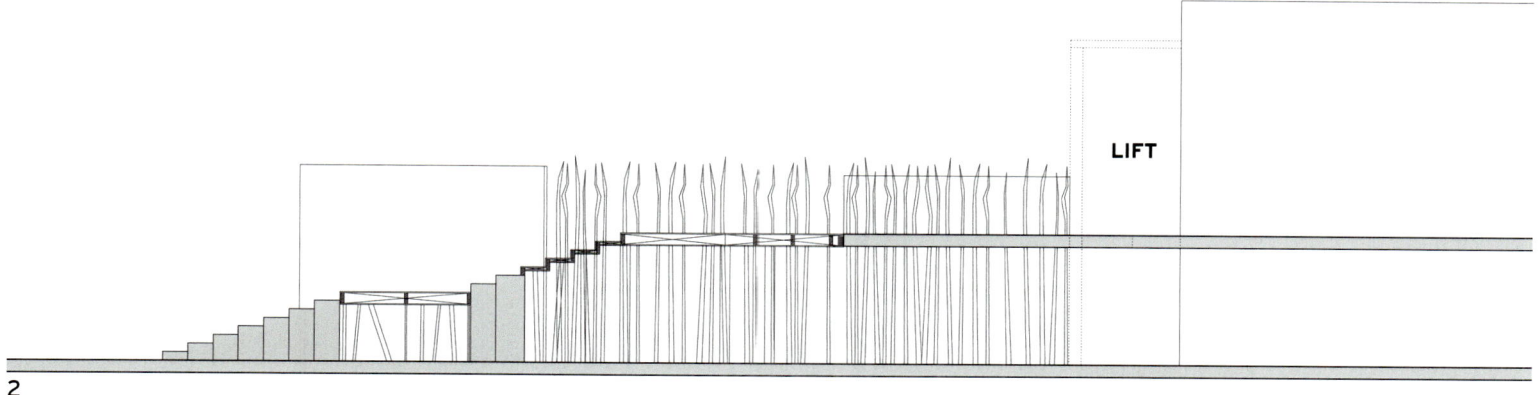

2

3

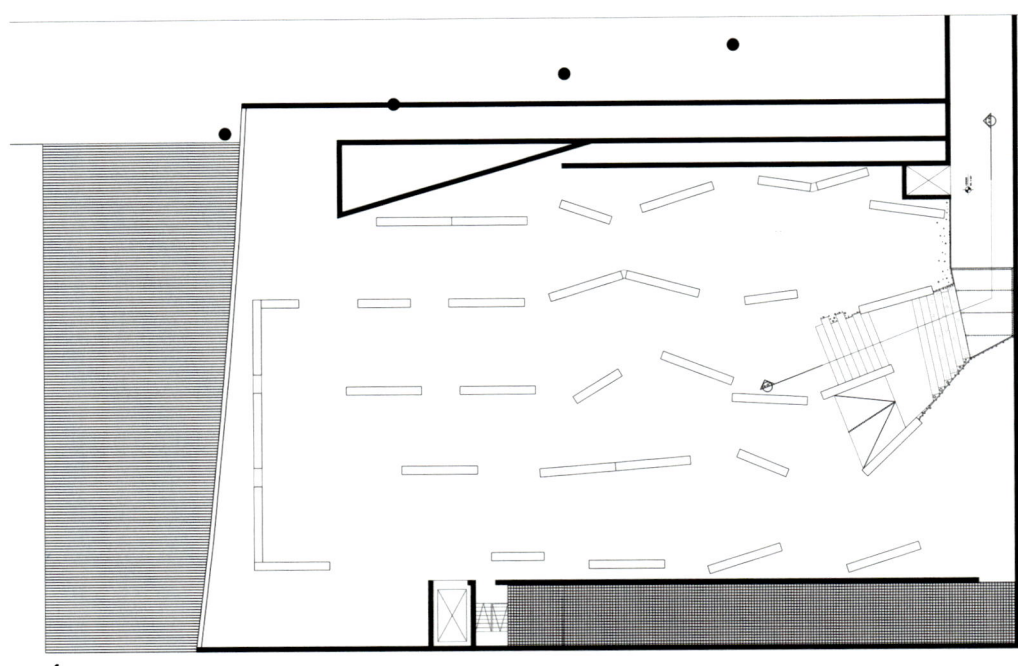

4

4 *Plan of exhibition*
5 *Detail with Lycra over elk's antler*
6 *Plan of exhibition*
7 *Concept drawing showing sightlines*
8 *View of street*

5

6

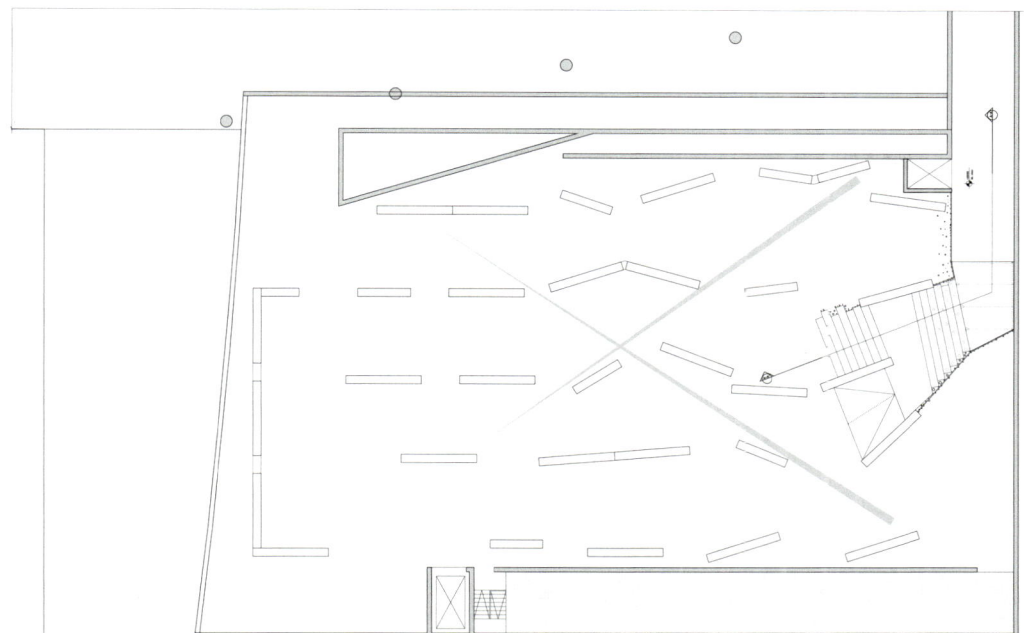

7

8

9

10

9&12   *View of street*
10   *Sightline*
11&13   *Detail of ramp at stair*
14   *Detail of stair*

11

12

13

14

15

15 *Lounge connecting Halls 2 and 3*
16 *Detail of classic room*
17 *Detail underneath stair*

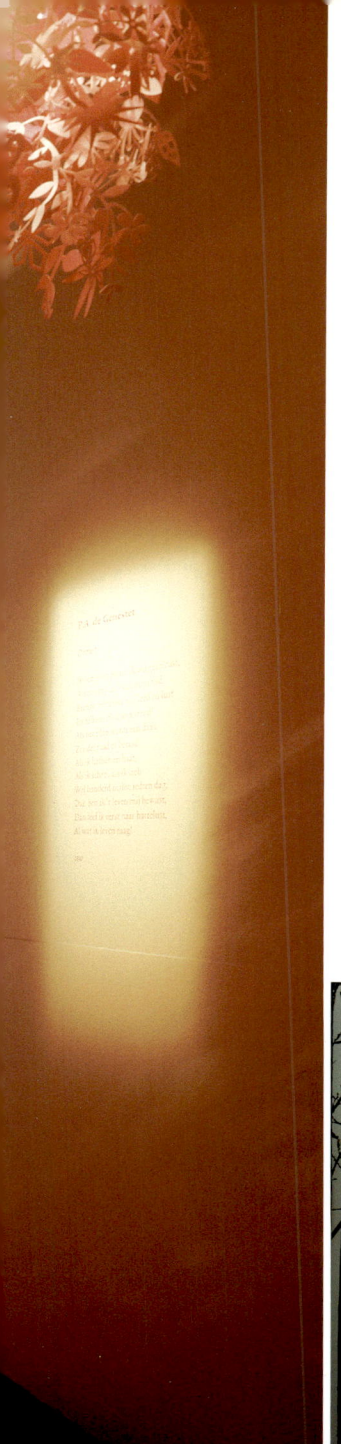

89

16

17

90

18

18&20 *Detail of wallpaper*
19 *View from top of stairs*
21 *Overall view of staircase*
22 *Sightline towards staircase*

19

20

21

22

CLIENT: Kunsthal Rotterdam, The Netherlands
DESIGN TEAM: Boris Zeisser, Maartje Lammers with Gerben Vos, Christianne Schets
DESIGN: 2006
CONSTRUCTION: 2006
FLOOR AREA: 1000 square metres

Dinosaurs Exhibition

KUNSTHAL, ROTTERDAM, THE NETHERLANDS

To accommodate the Dinosaurs Exhibition at the Kunsthal, the flexible walls of Kunsthal's Hall 1 were rearranged in a double abstract representation of a spine. This allowed the space to be reconfigured into three different zones to suit the exhibition.

The first space is fitted out as an abstract jungle, with a meandering path of thick, mushy rubber and vines made of cloth. The atmosphere is dark and mysterious; the walls are painted in a jungle-style pattern. Here are the moving animatronics to add to the atmosphere – including giant replica dinosaurs of all sorts, roaring and moving in the dim light.

In the eye of the two curved walls is a sacral night atmosphere, created for the skeleton of a gigantic Triceratops.

From here, visitors walk along the fossil graveyard towards the filtered daylight. Within the graveyard there is an abstract sandpit in which visitors can dig for dinosaur fossils like real paleontologists.

To enhance the entire exhibition, the glass façade, which takes in the view of the park as part of the exhibition, is covered with a translucent film showing a jungle collage. ■

1   *Triceratops under skeleton ceiling*

2

3

4

2 *Exterior view*
3 *Glass façade with jungle print*
4 *View towards park from behind the glass*
5 *Detail of jungle print on glass façade*

95

5

6

6 *Plan of exhibition*
7 *Exterior view*
8&9 *Triceratops details*
10 *Diplodocus skeleton*

7

8

9

10

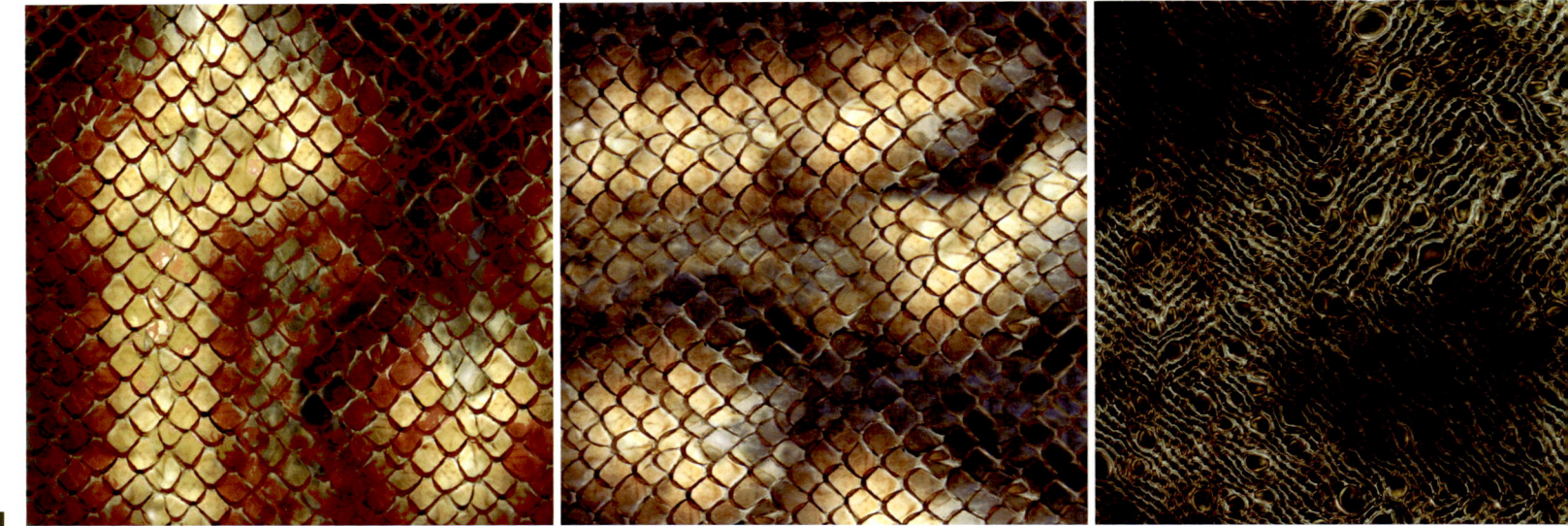

11

98

12

13

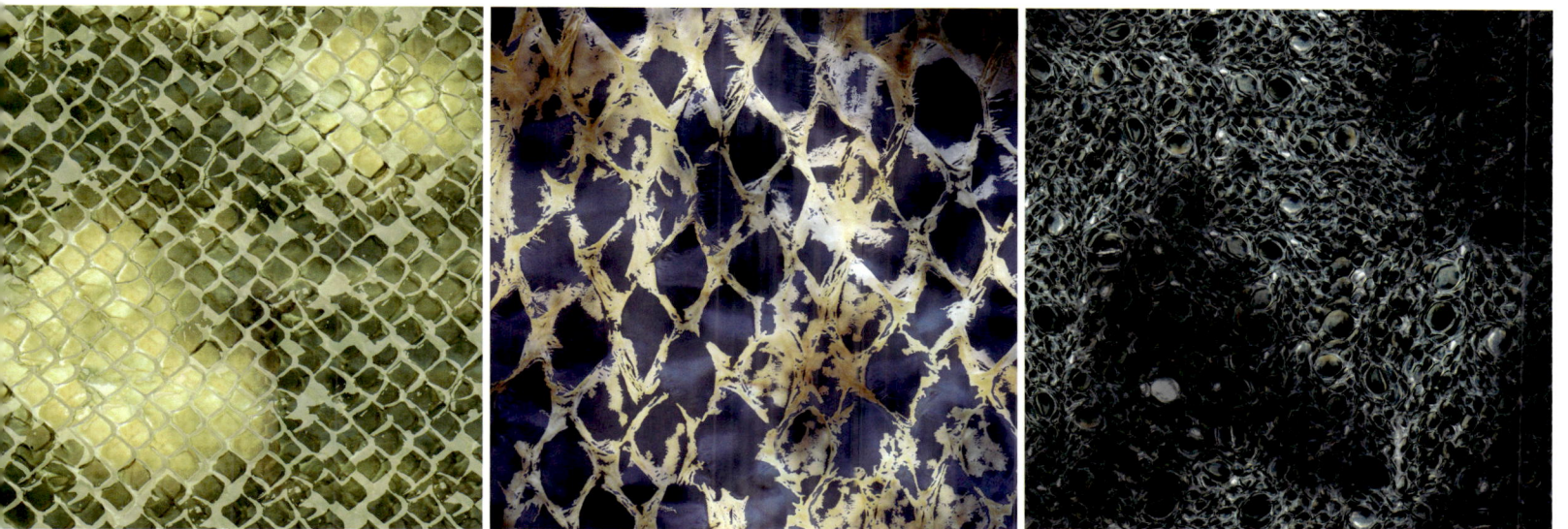

11 *Dinosaur skin wallpaper near sandpit*
12&13 *Animatronics in abstract jungle*
14 *View towards sandpit*

14

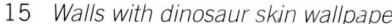

15 *Walls with dinosaur skin wallpaper*
16 *Abstract jungle painted walls behind*

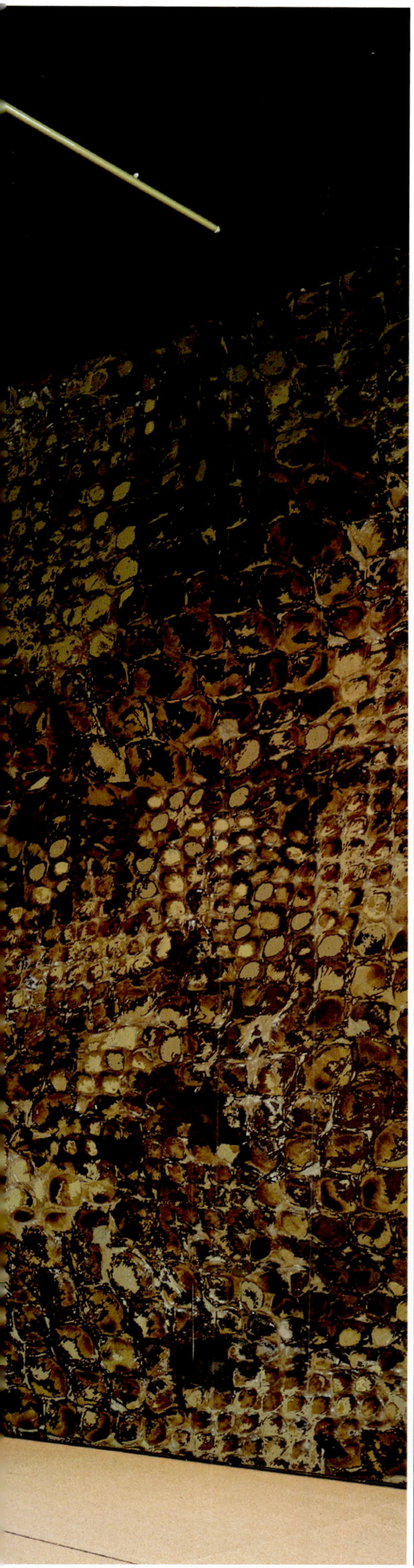

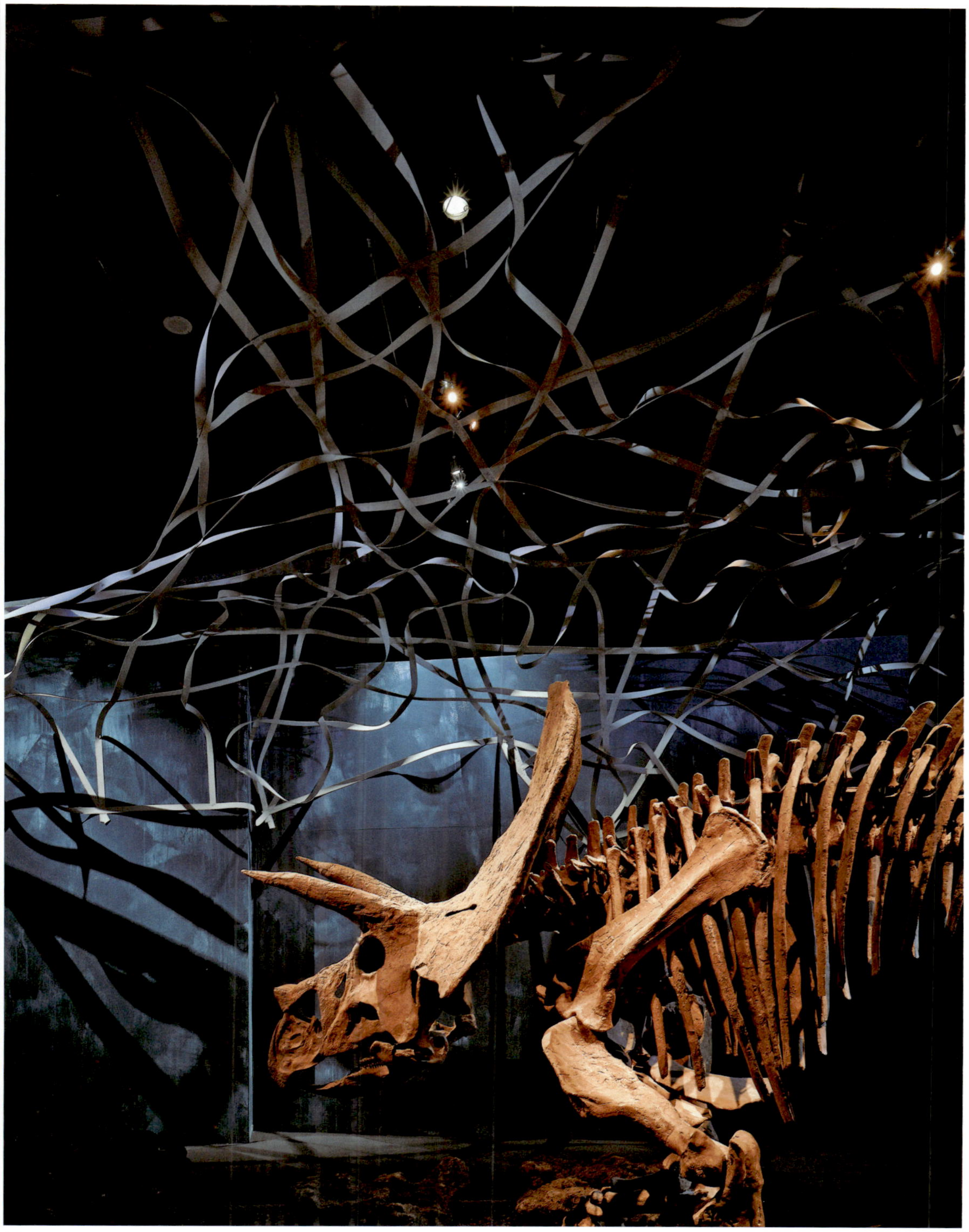

16

102

17

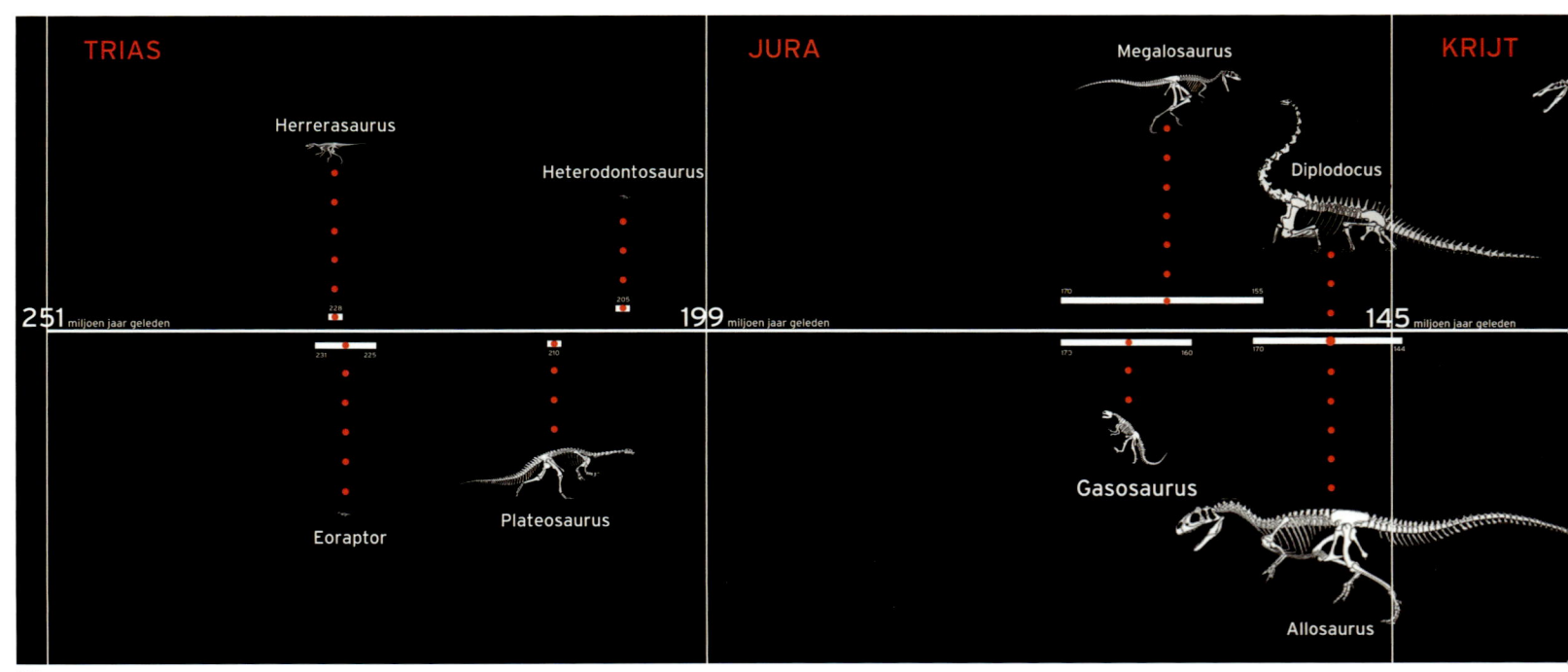

TRIAS	JURA		KRIJT

Herrerasaurus

Heterodontosaurus

Megalosaurus

Diplodocus

251 miljoen jaar geleden

199 miljoen jaar geleden

145 miljoen jaar geleden

228

205

231   225

210

170   155

173   160

170   144

Eoraptor

Plateosaurus

Gasosaurus

Allosaurus

18

19

20

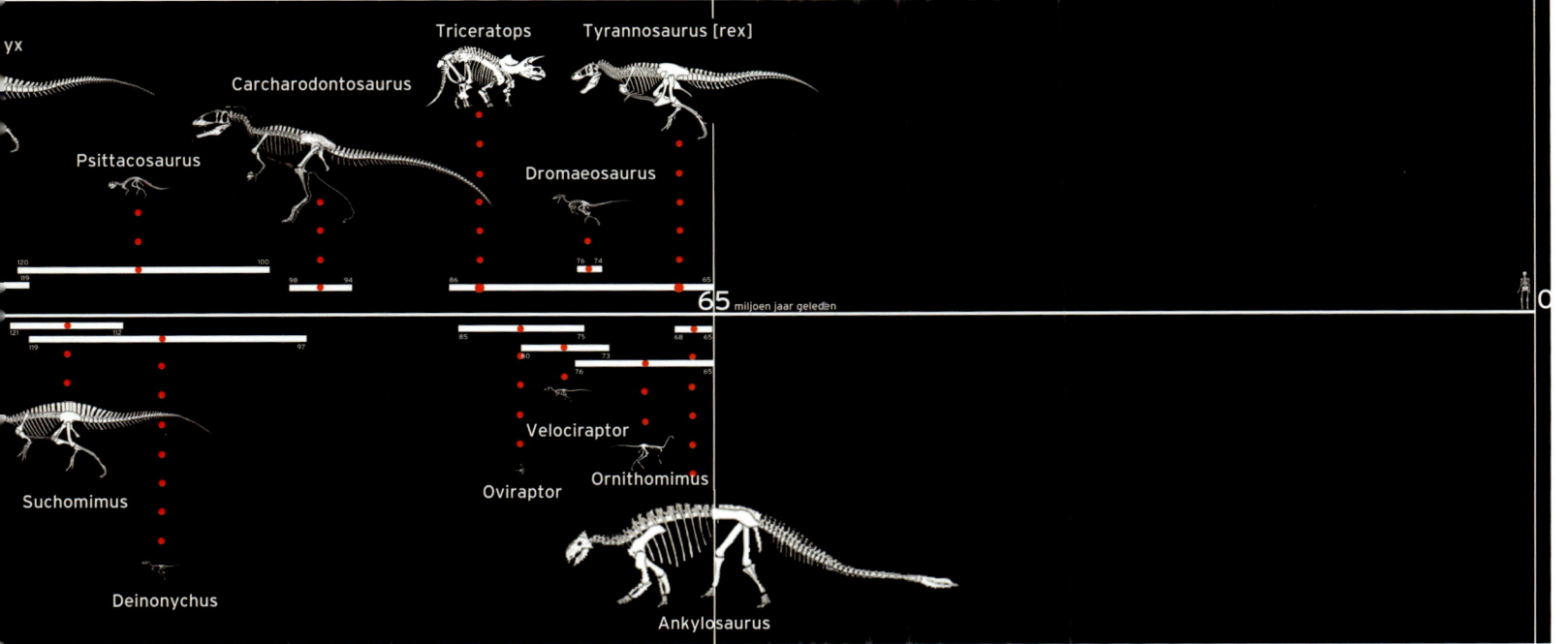

CLIENT: Hostels UK Ltd, London
ARCHITECT: Maartje Lammers, Boris Zeisser with Fieke Poelman, Gerben Vos, Ruben Bergambagt, Sandor Marks, Christianne Schets, Marloen Swijnenburg, Klasien Visser
DESIGN: 2006
CONSTRUCTION: 2006–2007
FLOOR AREA: 4000 square metres
BUILDING COST: €4 million

Courthouse Hostel

LONDON, ENGLAND

The firm is developing the interior for a design hostel located in a former courthouse in the centre of London. This historic building, which has listed interior spaces, is to be re-used as a 600-bed youth hostel.

The main issue is to make the building accessible and simple to navigate, and to create a clear design that allows people to get their bearings. Main corridors are connected as a ring structure, like a continuous ribbon under the ceiling, with secondary corridors leading from these rings. The different levels will have their own colour and thematic images on the ceiling ribbon, so that guests can find their way to their rooms using the vertical and horizontal cues.

Within the hostel there are several spaces that have their own particular atmosphere and interior design, such as the internet room, the lounge bar, the entrance area, the kitchen/dining room and the bar space.

Between 2 and 16 beds wil be placed in each bedroom, combined in single or bunk formats. Special elements will be integrated into the design of the beds to allow guests flexibility and independence. These include storage and safety boxes, lighting and privacy panels, which are fitted with images related to the particular theme on each level.

In the former courtrooms large structures are placed to accomodate internet lounge and seating areas in the bar, in enormous red 'insects'.

This design for the hostel adds a series of contemporary, user-friendly elements as well as a great atmosphere: everything you need in a home away from home. ■

1 *Section through courtrooms*
2 *Existing building*
3 *Section through entrance hall*

1

2

BEDROOM
INTERNET CAFE
LOUNGE BAR
DINING
BAR
SHERLOCK HOLMES

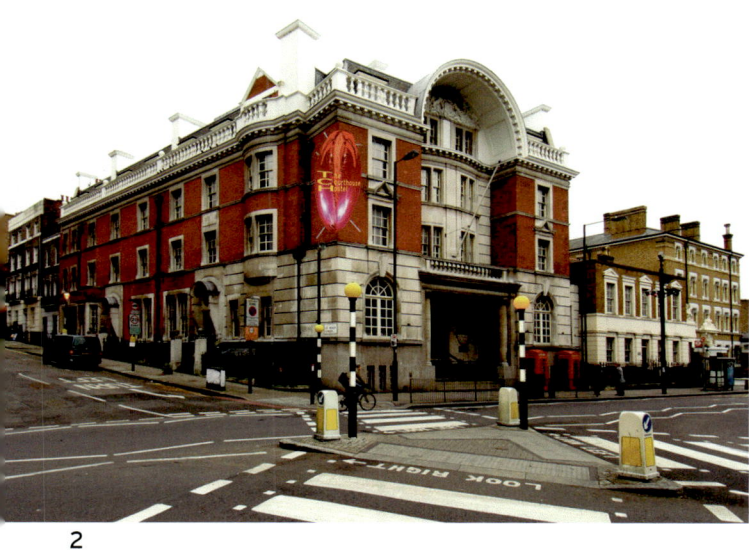

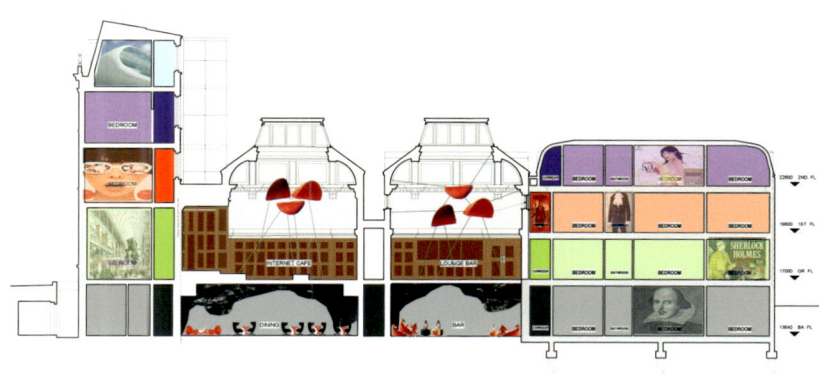

3

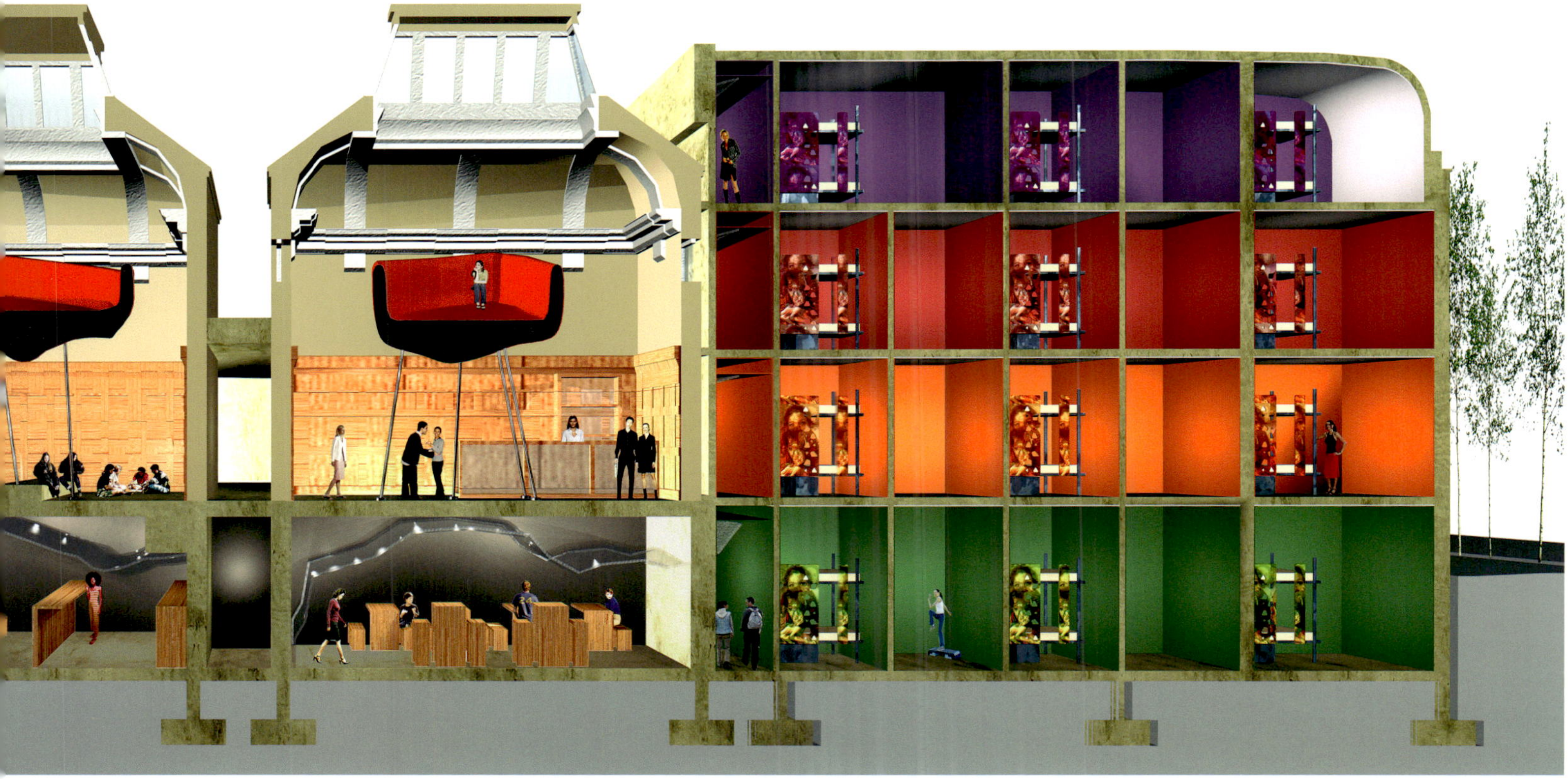

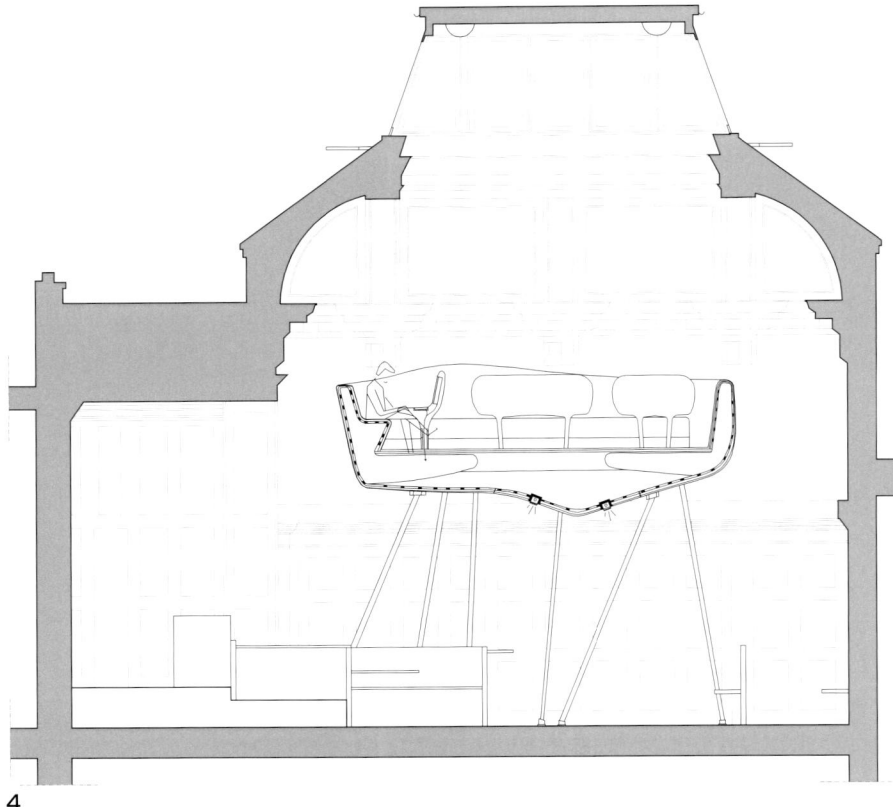

4

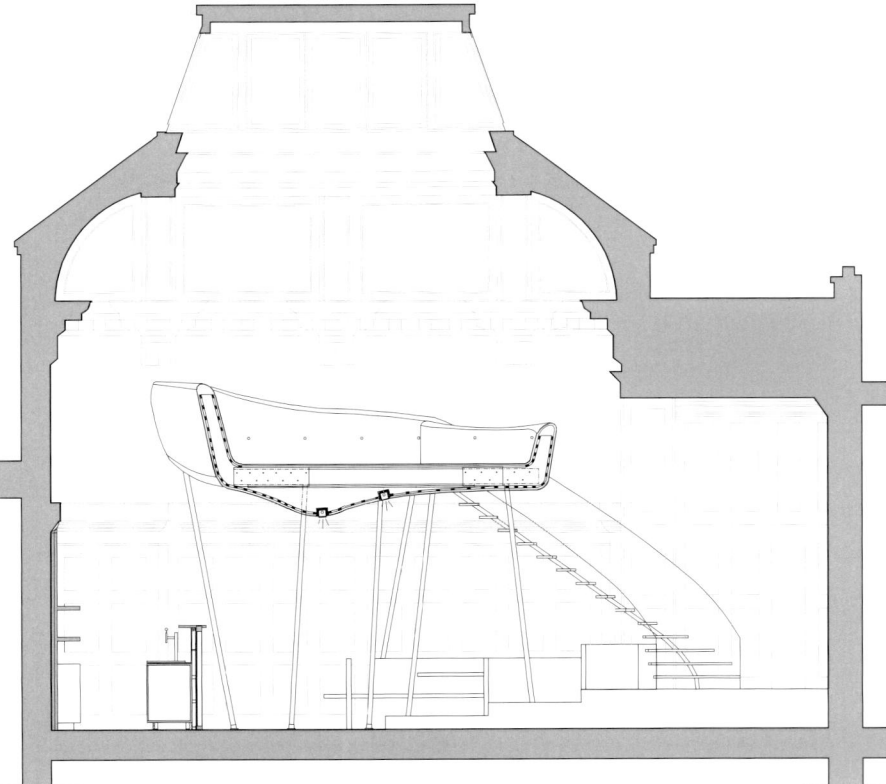

5

4 *Section through internet lounge in former courtroom*
5 *Section through bar in former courtroom*
6&7 *Bed pods have privacy screens with integrated ladder*

6

7

CLIENT: Wellness Bouw bv, Schiedam, The Netherlands
DESIGN TEAM: Maartje Lammers, Boris Zeisser with Peterine Arts, Dirk Zschunke,
	Sandor Marks, Ruben Bergambagt, Marloes Swijnenburg,
	Onat Oktem, Marta Koziol, Albert-Jan Vermeulen, Aggeliki Aggeli
CONSULTANTS: CAE structural engineers, Rotterdam, Hans Ketel
DESIGN: 2006–2007
CONSTRUCTON: 2007–2008
FLOOR AREA: 8830 square metres
COSTS: €9 million

Thermen Spa Haarlemmermeer

HOOFDDORP, THE NETHERLANDS

The Hoofddorp Thermen Spa – a substantial sauna complex that is reported to be the largest in the world – has taken a global approach to design by adopting the theme of 'A Tour Around the World'.

The challenge with this design was to create an abstract representation of the various countries without being kitsch.

The building itself is a stretched volume, with a large 'eye' overlooking the polder. The eye also provides the entrance to the complex at the first floor level.

The reception area, dressing rooms and beauty centre are located here, as are wide staircases that direct visitors into the sauna area.

A continuous pool, designed to be a fluid link throughout the building, changes shape constantly, depending on the country through which it passes. It is the one element that links all the themes together.

Outside, the gardens have been designed with little sauna cabins, each of which relates to the theme of the 'A Tour Around the World'. ∎

1	*Concept scheme of complex*
2	*Elevation of front with elevated baths*
3	*Elevation of back*
4	*Detail of baths façade*

1

2

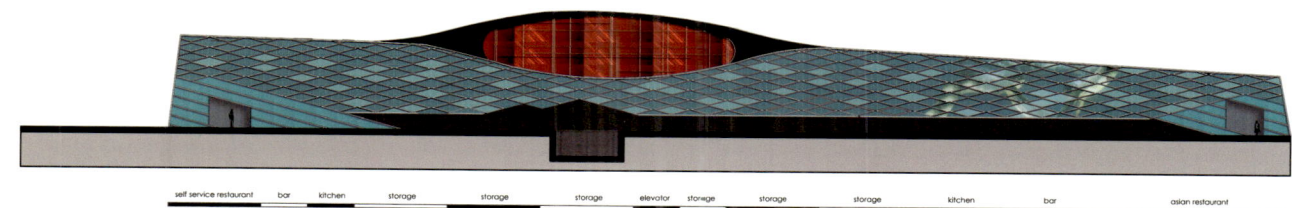

self service restaurant | bar | kitchen | storage | storage | storage | elevator | storage | storage | storage | kitchen | bar | asian restaurant

3

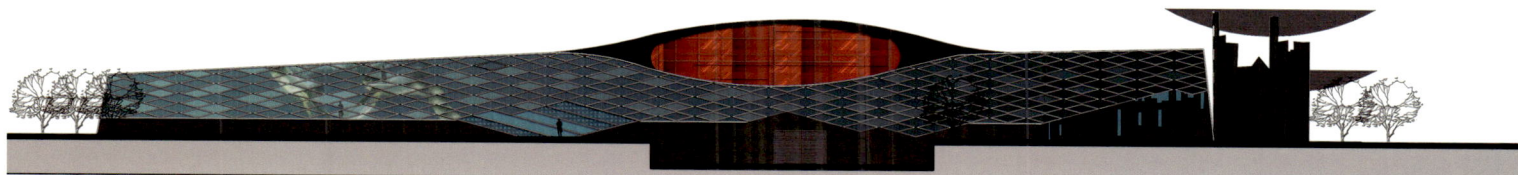

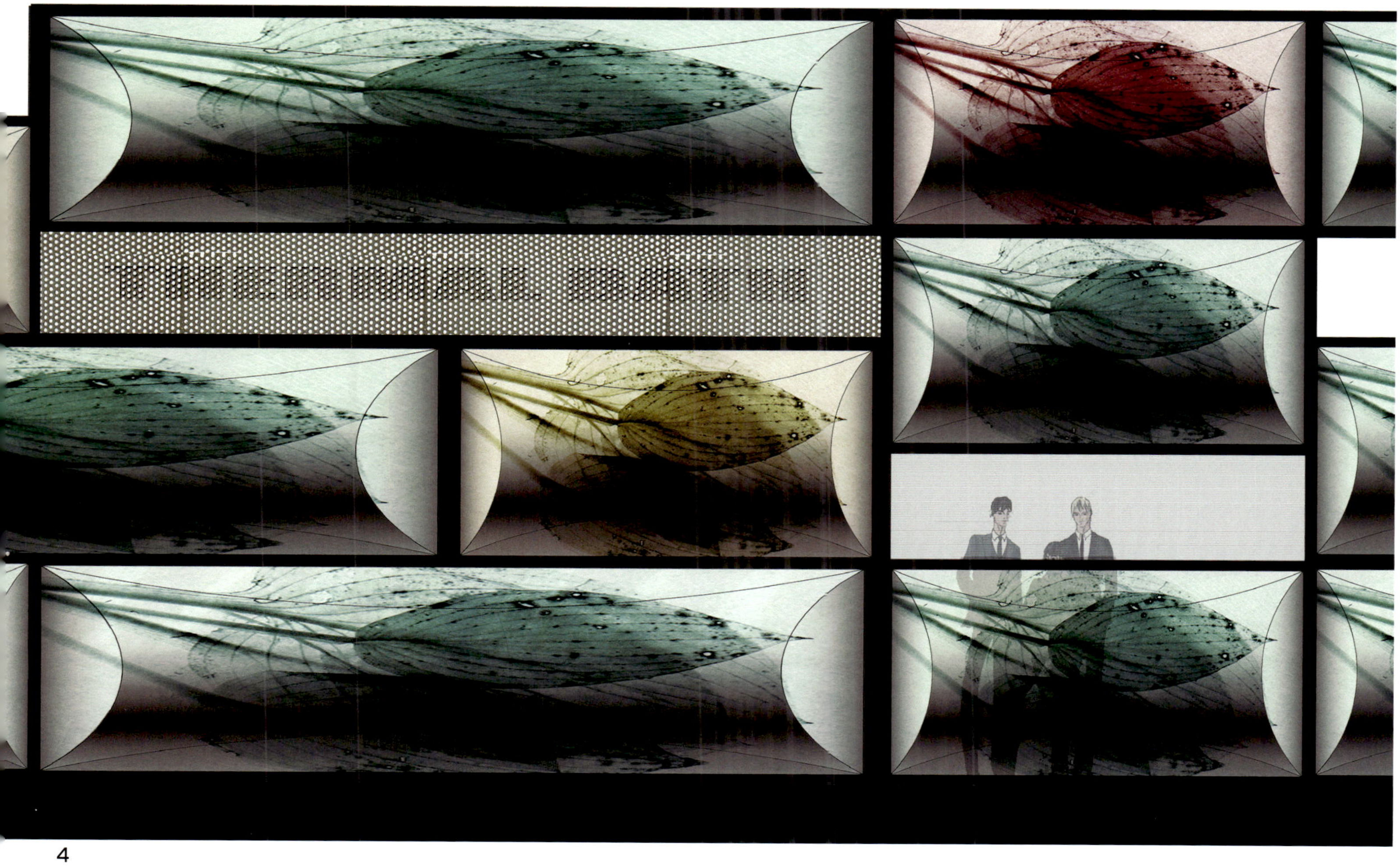

4

5

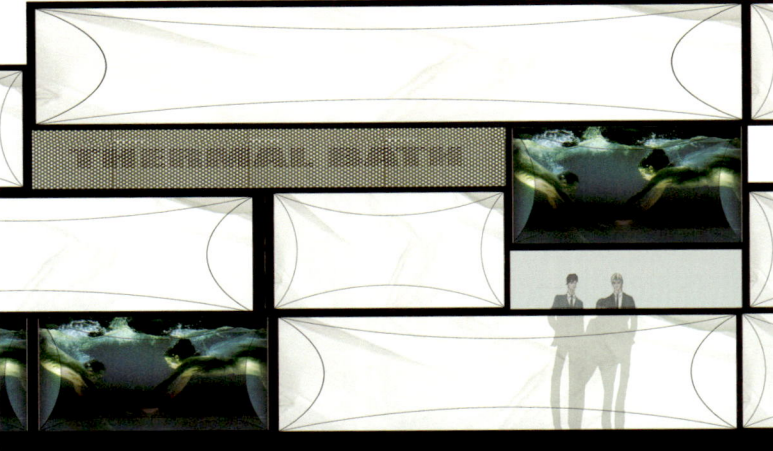

6

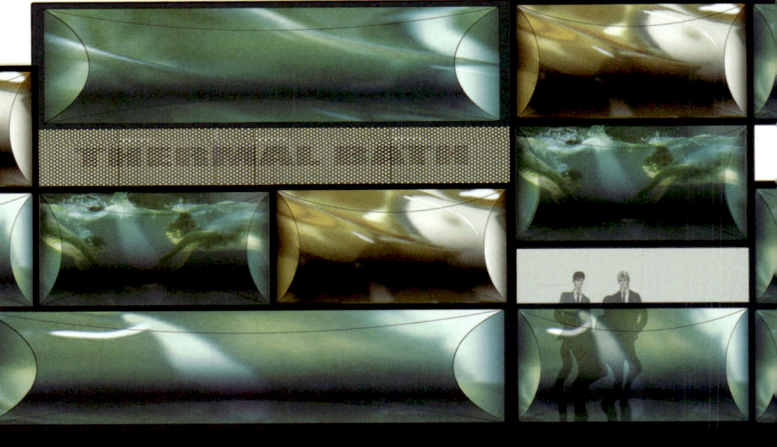

7

8

5 *Various outdoor sauna concepts*
6&7 *Studies of façade*
8 *Representation of 'A Tour around the World'*
9 *Side façade, higher end*
10 *Side façade, lower end*

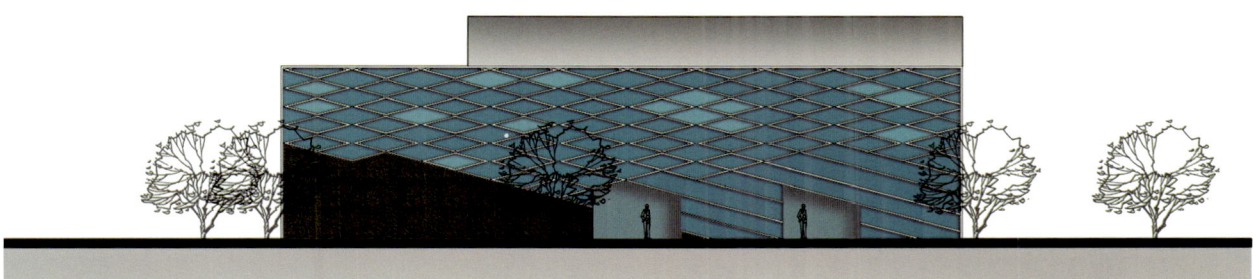

9

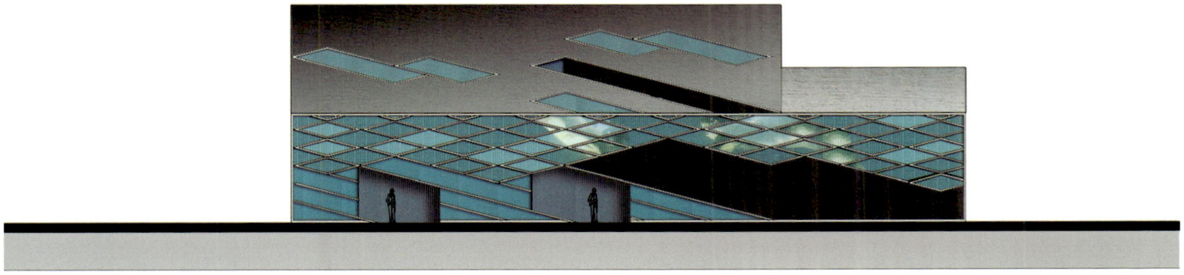

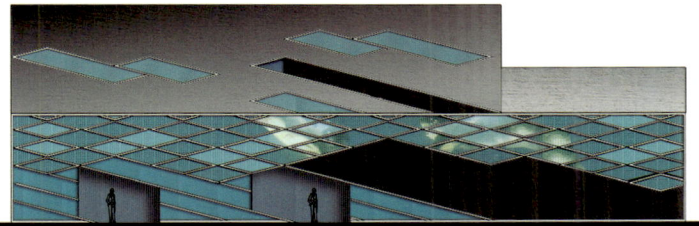

10

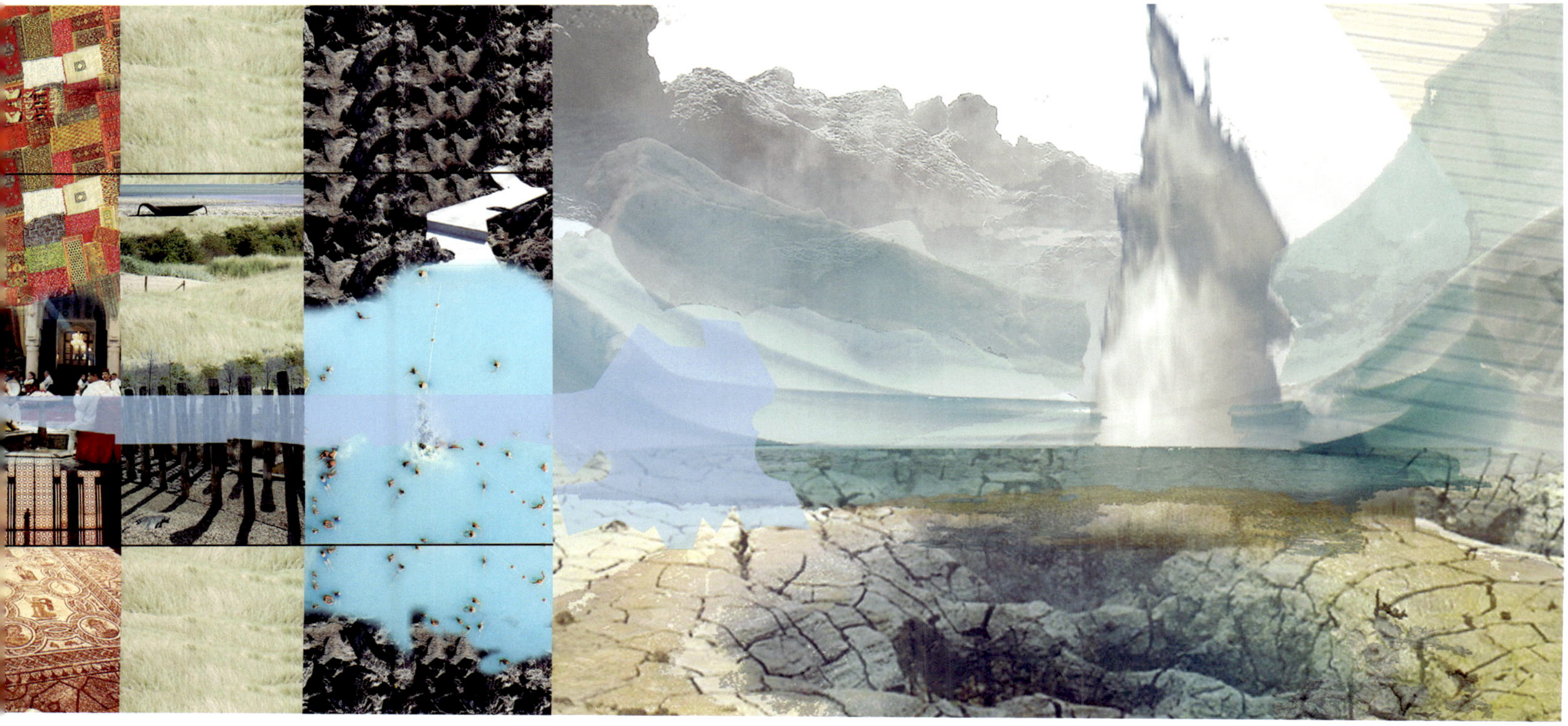

11

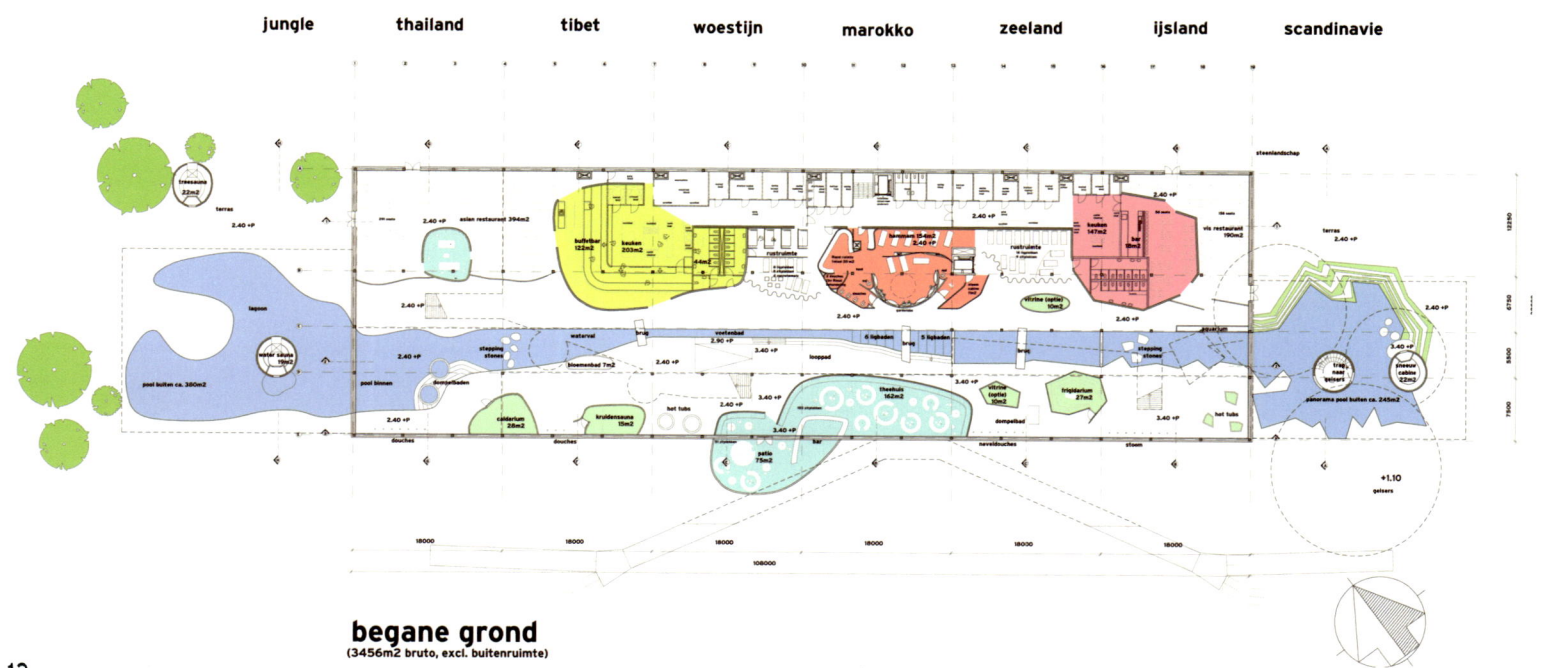

12

jungle	thailand	tibet	woestijn	marokko	zeeland	ijsland	scandinavie

begane grond
(3456m2 bruto, excl. buitenruimte)

13

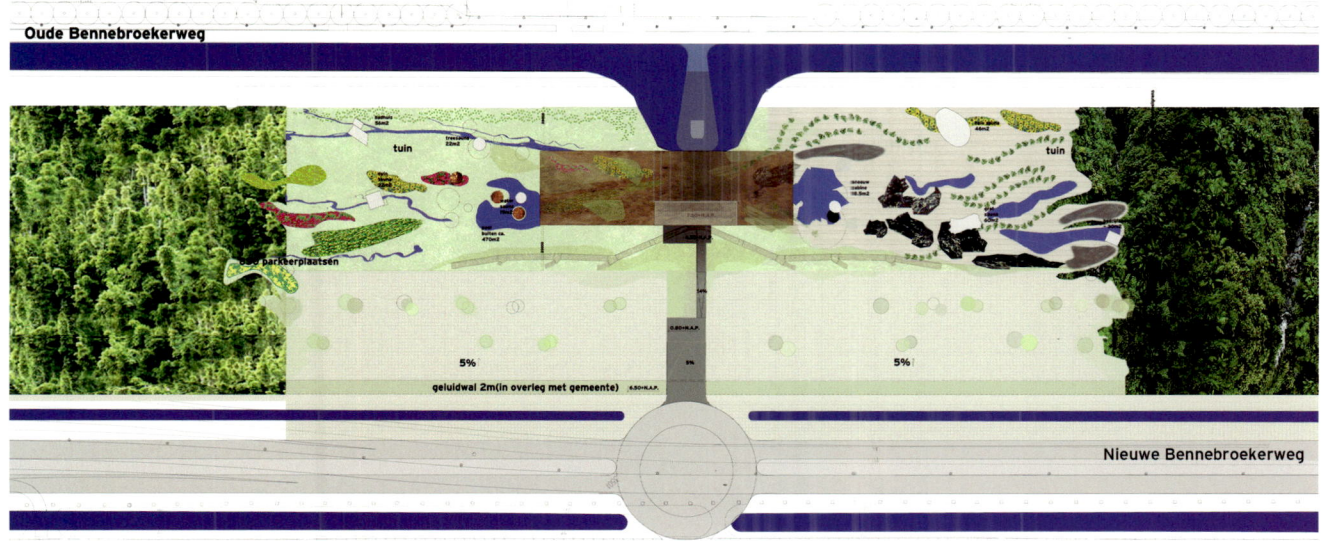

14

11 *Day view*
12 *Night view*
13 *Plan of ground-floor sauna/wellness area*
14 *Plan of garden*
15 *Detail of façade*

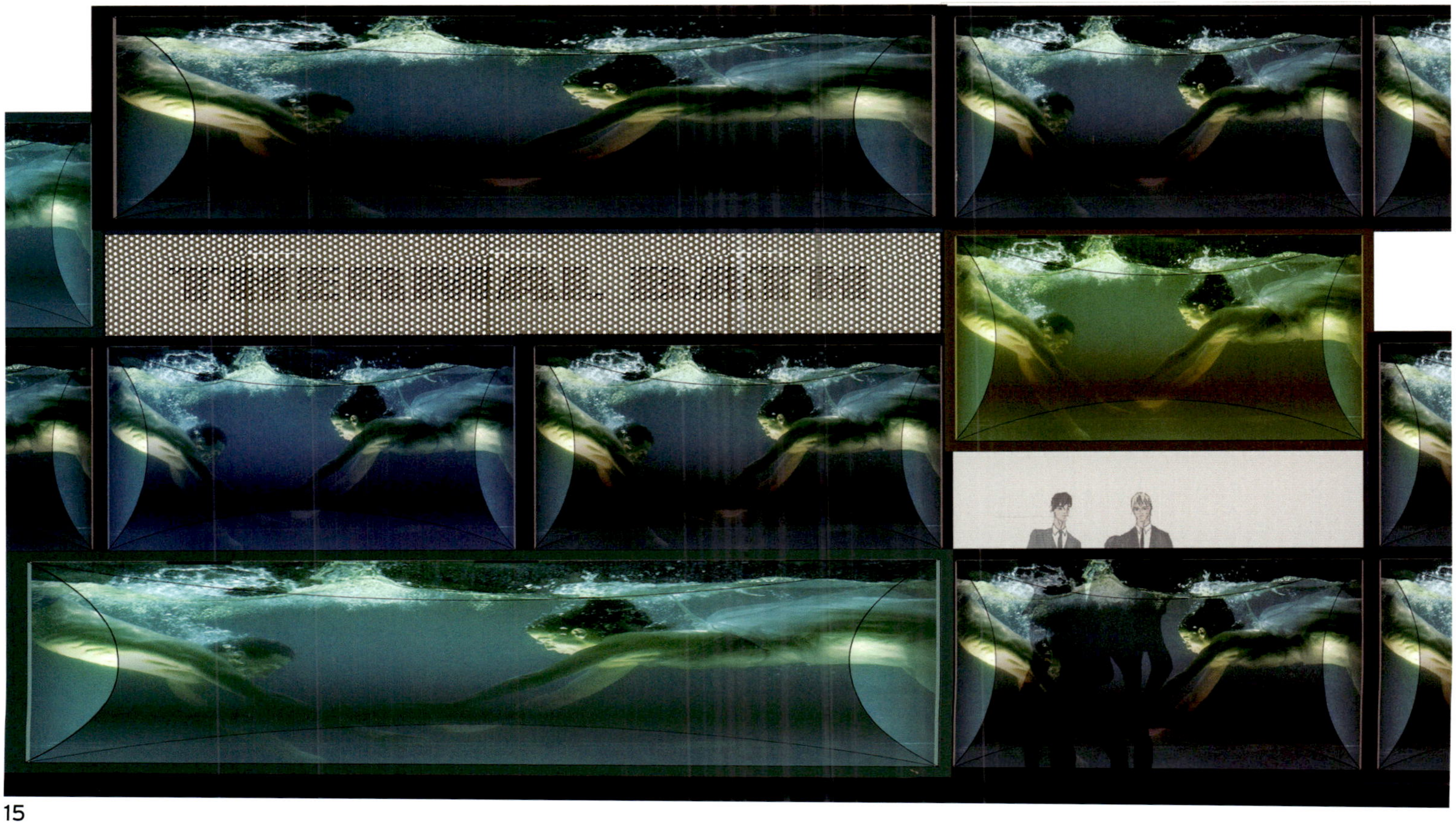

15

PROJECT CREDITS

ARTS PAVILION
Peckham, London, England
CLIENT: Municipality of Peckham, Camberwell Arts College
DESIGN TEAM: Boris Zeisser, Maartje Lammers with Ruben Bergambagt, Marie Allard Latour
DESIGN: 2005 (competition)
FLOOR AREA: 150 square metres
BUILDING COSTS: €350,000

ASHLEE HOUSE HOSTEL
London, England
CLIENT: Ashlee House London, Anne Dolan
DESIGN TEAM: Boris Zeisser, Maartje Lammers with Olav Bruin, Sabrina Kers, Gerben Vos
DESIGN: 2002–2003
CONSTRUCTION: 2003
FLOOR AREA: 200 square metres
BUILDING COSTS: €22,000

BEACH PAVILION
Zeeland, Flanders, The Netherlands
CLIENT: Municipality of Sluis, Tiny Maenhout
DESIGN TEAM: Boris Zeisser, Maartje Lammers with Olav Bruin, Wouter Homs
DESIGN: 2003
FLOOR AREA: 200 square metres
BUILDING COSTS: €400,000

COURTHOUSE HOSTEL
London, England
CLIENT: Hostels UK Ltd. London, John F. Dolan
DESIGN TEAM: Maartje Lammers, Boris Zeisser with Fieke Poelman, Gerben Vos, Ruben Bergambagt, Sandor Marks, Christianne Schets, Marloes Swijnenburg, Klasien Visser
DESIGN: 2006
CONSTRUCTION: 2006–2007
FLOOR AREA: 4000 square metres
BUILDING COSTS: €4 million

DINOSAURS EXHIBITION
Rotterdam, The Netherlands
CLIENT: Kunsthal, Rotterdam, Wim Pijbes
DESIGN TEAM: Maartje Lammers, Boris Zeisser with Gerben Vos, Christianne Schets
CONSULTANTS: Bart Cuppens
DESIGN: 2006
CONSTRUCTION: 2006
FLOOR AREA: 1000 square metres

DRAGSPELHUSET SUMMER HOUSE
Lake Övre Gla, Sweden
CLIENT: Zeisser
DESIGN TEAM: Boris Zeisser, Maartje Lammers with Olav Bruin, Jeroen ter Haar, Séverine Kas, Sabrina Kers, Fieke Poelman, Ingrid Owens, Sandor Marks and Ruben Bergambagt
ENGINEERS: ABT Consultants, Delft and Marcus Lorenz, Exmouth, Australia
DESIGN: 2001–2002
CONSTRUCTION: 2002–2004
FLOOR AREA: 54–72 square metres
BUILDING COSTS: €80,000

ECO SPECIALS, SONEVA KIRI RESORT
Koh Kut, Thailand
CLIENT: Six Senses, Bangkok, Sonu Shivdasani
DESIGN TEAM: Boris Zeisser, Maartje Lammers with Olav Bruin, Dirk Zschunke, Marta Koziol and Marloes Swijnenburg
DESIGN: 2006–2007
CONSTRUCTION: 2007
FLOOR AREA: 500 square metres
BUILDING COSTS: €800,000

ELEMENTARY SCHOOL COMPLEX
Haarlemmermeer, The Netherlands
CLIENT: Municipality of Haarlemmermeer,
Fred Kaaij
DESIGN TEAM: Maartje Lammers, Boris Zeisser with
Heleen Bothof, Jeroen ter Haar, Sabrina Kers
DESIGN: 2002 (competition)
FLOOR AREA: 5600 square metres
BUILDING COSTS: €5.2 million

FASHION CAVE
Salzburg, Austria
CLIENT: Aco Mode Agentur, Vienna, Rudolf Kail
DESIGN TEAM: Maartje Lammers, Boris Zeisser with
Michele Stramezzi, Saman Saffarian, Ruben
Bergambagt, Sylvain Grasset
CONSULTANTS: Van der Plas interiors
DESIGN: 2004–2005
CONSTRUCTION: delayed
FLOOR AREA: 900 square metres
BUILDING COSTS: €300,000

FLORIANDE ISLAND 7 HOUSING
Hoofddorp, The Netherlands
CLIENT: Ymere, Amsterdam, Betty Oderkerk
DESIGN TEAM: Boris Zeisser, Maartje Lammers with
Gerben Vos, Sabrina Kers, Fieke Poelman, Wouter
Homs, Olav Bruin, Nora Rittmüller, Sylvain Grasset,
Christian Schultze
ENGINEERS: ABT Consultants, Delft
DESIGN: 2003–2004
CONSTRUCTION: 2005–2006
FLOOR AREA: 7200 square metres
BUILDING COSTS: €5.2 million

FLORIANDE ISLAND 7 SEMI-DETACHED HOUSING
Hoofddorp, The Netherlands
CLIENT: AM wonen, Albert Groothuizen
DESIGN TEAM: Boris Zeisser, Maartje Lammers with
Fieke Poelman, Gerben Vos, Nora Rittmüller,
Sabrina Kers, Sandra Vergin
DESIGN: 2003–2004
CONSTRUCTION: 2005–2006
FLOOR AREA: 35 houses
BUILDING COSTS: €4.5 million

FORMER CHURCH (REFURBISHMENT)
Purmerend, The Netherlands
CLIENT: Mieneke van Gogh
DESIGN TEAM: Maartje Lammers, Boris Zeisser with
Jeroen ter Haar, Amelie Kaltenbach, Ingrid Owens
DESIGN: 2002–2003
FLOOR AREA: 850 square metres
BUILDING COSTS: €1.3 million

GETSEWOUD HOUSING
Nieuw Vennep, The Netherlands
CLIENT: Ymere, Betty Oderkerk
DESIGN TEAM: Boris Zeisser, Maartje Lammers with
Gerben Vos, Heleen Bothof, Sabrina Kers,
Jeroen ter Haar, Ingrid Owens
ENGINEERS: ABT Consultants
DESIGN: 2001–2002
CONSTRUCTION: 2003
FLOOR AREA: 4500 square metres
BUILDING COSTS: €3.6 million

HOOFDDORP HOUSING AND SHOPS
Hoofddorp, The Netherlands
CLIENT: Aprisco, Assen, Harold Beugelink
DESIGN TEAM: Maartje Lammers, Boris Zeisser with
Gerben Vos, Sabrina Kers, Casper de Heer,
Sabine Simon, Christian Schultze
DESIGN: 2005–2006, on hold
FLOOR AREA: 38 apartments and commercial space
BUILDING COSTS: €5.8 million

HYBRID HOUSING COMPLEX
Smitsveen Park, Soest, The Netherlands
CLIENT: Portaal
DESIGN TEAM: Boris Zeisser and Maartje Lammers
with Saman Saffarian, Bruno Toledo
DESIGN: 2005, on hold
FLOOR AREA: 40,000 square metres
BUILDING COSTS: €36 million

ICHTHUS ACADEMY
Rotterdam, The Netherlands
CLIENT: Ichthus Academy, Jan de Vries
DESIGN TEAM: Maartje Lammers, Boris Zeisser with
Jeroen ter Haar, Heleen Bothof, Séverine Kas
Sabrina Kers, Gerben Vos, Ingrid Owens
CONSULTANTS: BAM Techniek
DESIGN: 2001
CONSTRUCTION: 2001–2002
FLOOR AREA: 1800 square metres
BUILDING COSTS: €680,000

KENNEMER GASTHUIS MASTERPLAN
Haarlem, The Netherlands
CLIENT: BAM NBM Vastgoed, Delta Lloyd Vastgoed
& Thunnissen Ontwikkeling
DESIGN TEAM: Maartje Lammers, Boris Zeisser with
Jeroen ter Haar, Heleen Bothof, Sabrina Kers,
Fieke Poelman, Olav Bruin
COMPETITION: 2001
FLOOR AREA: 30,000 square metres
BUILDING COSTS: €30 million

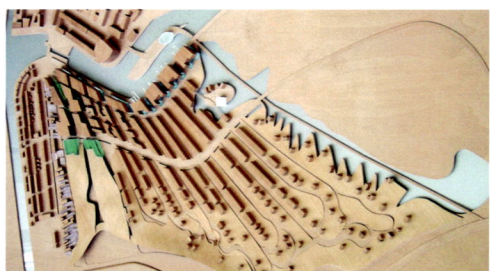

KOP VAN WEST MASTERPLAN
Purmerend, The Netherlands
CLIENT: MAB, I. Kalisvaart
DESIGN TEAM: Maartje Lammers, Boris Zeisser with
Heleen Bothof, Séverine Kas, Fieke Poelman,
Amelie Kaltenbach and Sabrina Kers
DESIGN: 2001-2003
FLOOR AREA: 200,000 square metres
BUILDING COSTS: €200 million

MART VISSER STORE
LOCATION: various
CLIENT: Mart Visser, Zantman Modegroep
Amsterdam, Pascale Zantman
DESIGN TEAM: Maartje Lammers, Boris Zeisser with
Heleen Bothof, Gerben Vos, Jeroen ter Haar,
Sandra Vergin
CONSULTANTS: Vizona Diemen
DESIGN: 2002, on hold

**'MEESTERS VAN DE ROMANTIEK' ('ROMANTIC
MOVEMENT') EXHIBITION**
Kunsthal Museum, Rotterdam, The Netherlands
CLIENT: Kunsthal Rotterdam, Wim Pijbes
DESIGN TEAM: Maartje Lammers, Boris Zeisser with
Michele Stramezzi, Nora Rittmuller
CONSULTANTS: Bart Cuppens
DESIGN: 2005
CONSTRUCTION: 2005
FLOOR AREA: 2000 square metres

MULTIFUNCTIONAL BUILDING
Böblingen, Germany
CLIENT: Böblinger Baugesellschaft
DESIGN TEAM: Boris Zeisser, Maartje Lammers with
Jeroen ter Haar, Amelie Kaltenbach, Olav Bruin and
Fieke Poelman
DESIGN: 2002 (competition)
FLOOR AREA: 4500 square metres
BUILDING COSTS: €7.6 million

MULTIFUNCTIONAL BUILDING
Hoofddorp, The Netherlands
CLIENT: Dura Vermeer Vastgoed, Zoetermeer, Erwin
Wessels
DESIGN TEAM: Maartje Lammers, Boris Zeisser with
Gerben Vos, Fieke Poelman, Peterine Arts,
Bruno Toledo, Sandor Marks, Amelie Kaltenbach,
Wouter Homs, Susan Hoekstra, Nora Rittmüller,
Marta Koziol
DESIGN: 2004–2007
FLOOR AREA: 60,000 square metres (mixed use and
parking garage)
BUILDING COSTS: €65 million

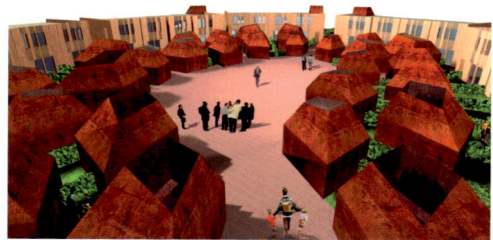

MUSICIANS' HOUSING
Hoogvliet, The Netherlands
CLIENT: Estrade projecten, Joost Lobee
DESIGN TEAM: Maartje Lammers, Boris Zeisser with
Gerben Vos, Amelie Kaltenbach, Albert-Jan
Vermeulen, Sandor Marks, Nora Rittmüller
DESIGN: 2006–2007
CONSTRUCTION: 2007–2008
FLOOR AREA: 38 houses and music rooms
BUILDING COSTS: €3.1 million

PUMPSTATION ZEEBURG
Amsterdam, The Netherlands
CLIENT: DWR
DESIGN TEAM: Maartje Lammers, Boris Zeisser with
Jeroen ter Haar, Amelie Kaltenbach, Ingrid Owens
DESIGN: 2002 (competition, 2nd prize)
FLOOR AREA: 500 square metres
BUILDING COSTS: €700,000

SCHOTERBURCHT HOUSING
Haarlem, The Netherlands
CLIENT: Municipality of Haarlem, Johan Matser
Project Development
DESIGN TEAM: Boris Zeisser and Maartje Lammers
with Penney Nourney, Wouter Homs and Olav Bruin
DESIGN: 2004 (competition, 2nd prize)
FLOOR AREA: 1200 square metres
BUILDING COSTS: €1.5 million

SCIENCEPARK HOUSING
Amsterdam, The Netherlands
CLIENT: Heddes Vastgoed, Hoorn, Paul Nijhout
DESIGN TEAM: Boris Zeisser, Maartje Lammers with Fieke Poelman, Gerben Vos, Sabrina Kers, Susan Hoekstra, Olav Bruin, Saman Saffarian, Jacopo van der Horst, Nora Rittmüller, Marie Allard Latour, Sandor Marks, Ben de Lange, Klasien Visser, Arnout Verweij, Sarah van Apeldoorn, Sabine Simon
ENGINEERS: ABT Consultants, Delft/Velp, Peutz Zoetermeer, Ilex Installation Management, Nieuwegein
DESIGN: 2004–2007
CONSTRUCTION: 2007–2008
FLOOR AREA: 87 apartments and parking garage
BUILDING COSTS: €14 million

SNOW CASTLE
Jevnaker, Norway
CLIENT: Steinerskolen Ringerike, Henrik Thaulow
DESIGN TEAM: Maartje Lammers, Boris Zeisser with Olav Bruin
DESIGN: 2006
CONSTRUCTION: 2006
FLOOR AREA: 100 square metres
BUILDING COSTS: €10,000

SPINNING MILL CONVERSION
LOCATION: Enschede, The Netherlands
CLIENT: Gemeente Enschede, Maarten Rol
DESIGN TEAM: Maartje Lammers, Boris Zeisser with Albert-Jan Vermeulen, Gerben Vos, Fieke Poelman, Susan Hoekstra, Casper de Heer, Blandine Roulet
DESIGN: 2004–2005
CONSTRUCTION: 2006–2007
FLOOR AREA: 17,000 square metres
BUILDING COSTS: €10 million

THERMEN SPA BOEDHA SLUIS
LOCATION: Sluis, The Netherlands
CLIENT: Wellness Bouw bv, Tonny Gajadin
DESIGN TEAM: Maartje Lammers, Boris Zeisser with Peterine Arts, Marie Allard Latour
DESIGN: 2006–2007
CONSTRUCTION: 2007–2008
FLOOR AREA: 5700 square metres
BUILDING COSTS: €5 million

THERMEN SPA HAARLEMMERMEER
Hoofddorp, The Netherlands
CLIENT: Wellness Bouw bv, Tonny Gajadin
DESIGN TEAM: Maartje Lammers, Boris Zeisser with Peterine Arts, Albert-Jan Vermeulen, Dirk Zschunke, Sandor Marks, Gerben Vos, Ruben Bergambagt, Marloes Swijnenburg, Onat Oktem, Marta Koziol
CONSULTANTS: CAE structural engineers, Rotterdam, Hans Ketel
DESIGN: 2006–2007
CONSTRUCTION: 2007–2008
FLOOR AREA: 8830 square metres
BUILDING COSTS: €9 million

WALDORF SCHOOL
Rotterdam, The Netherlands
CLIENT: Rudolf Steiner College, Rudolf van Lierop
DESIGN TEAM: Boris Zeisser, Maartje Lammers with Amelie Kaltenbach, Carlyn Timmermans, Klasien Visser, Dirk Zschunke
CONSTRUCTION: 2009
FLOOR AREA: 7000 square metres
BUILDING COSTS: €6 million

WATERTOWER (REFURBISHMENT OF FORMER TOWER)
Domburg, The Netherlands
CLIENT: De Bruin, Klerks, Bilthoven
DESIGN TEAM: Maartje Lammers, Boris Zeisser with Sabrina Kers, Casper de Heer, Ruben Bergambagt, Gerben Vos and Olav Bruin
DESIGN: 2004–2006
CONSTRUCTION: 2007–2008
FLOOR AREA: 640 square metres
BUILDING COSTS: €960,000

YOUTH CLUB
Hoofddorp, The Netherlands
CLIENT: Municipality of Haarlemmermeer
DESIGN TEAM: Boris Zeisser, Maartje Lammers with Sabrina Kers
DESIGN: 2003–2004
FLOOR AREA: 600 square metres
BUILDING COSTS: €420,000

ZEEBURGER ISLAND (URBAN STUDY)
Amsterdam, The Netherlands
CLIENT: Municipality of Amsterdam
DESIGN TEAM: Maartje Lammers, Boris Zeisser with Amelie Kaltenbach and Olav Bruin
DESIGN: 2002
FLOOR AREA: 500 low-rise high-density housing
BUILDING COSTS: €50 million

BIOGRAPHIES

Maartje Lammers was born in 1963 and graduated from TU Delft (Delft University of Technology in The Netherlands) in 1988. Boris Zeisser was born in 1968 and graduated from TU Delft with honourable mention in 1995. Before starting their own office both partners worked at several well-known architectural offices, including the Office for Metropolitan Architecture (Rem Koolhaas), Mecanoo, and (EEA) Erick van Egeraat associated architects. Some of the noted projects they were both involved with, particularly at EEA, include the Ichthus Hogeschool in Rotterdam, the Crawford Municipal Art Gallery in Cork, Poppodium Mezz in Breda, the ING/Nationale Nederlanden head office in Budapest and the urban development of Oosterdoks Eiland in Amsterdam.

On January 1, 2001 (01.01.01), Boris and Maartje founded 24H architecture in Rotterdam. Its goal was, and is, to make evolutionary architecture of extreme quality and sensitivity. As such, their designs adapt themselves to the ever-changing parameters of 21st century society while still reflecting a layer of softness and sensitivity.

Since its inception 24H architecture has been involved in various projects, from large-scale to smaller and more private projects. Recently, a number of projects have been realised, with outstanding results, among them the Ichthus Academy in Rotterdam, the hotel lobby for Ashlee House in London, the Dragspelhuset at Övre Gla, Sweden, several exhibitions and various housing projects in both Nieuw Vennep and Hoofddorp in The Netherlands.

The international 16-person team of 24H currently works on a broad scope of design tasks, including several urban design projects, housing projects in Nijmegen, Hoogvliet, Hoofddorp and Amsterdam, a fashion cave in Salzburg, two schools in Rotterdam and Norrköping, Sweden, a hotel in London, England, an eco resort on the island of Koh Kood in Thailand, two large spa complexes in The Netherlands and the refurbishment of both a former spinning mill into offices (Enschede) and an old water tower into apartments (Domburg).

Maartje Lammers

1963	Born in Assen, The Netherlands
1982–1988	Technical University Delft, Faculty of Architecture
1988–1990	(OMA) Office for Metropolitan Architecture, Rotterdam
1990–1995	Mecanoo Architecten, Delft
1995–2000	(EEA) Erick van Egeraat Associated Architects, Rotterdam
2001–present	24H Architecture, Rotterdam

Teaching/Lectures

1994	Centre de Cultura Contemporana, Barcelona
1995–2006	Technical University, Delft
1997–2006	Academie voor Bouwkunst, Rotterdam
1999	University of Strasbourg

Committees

1995–2002	Member of the committee of Welstand & Monumenten, Rotterdam
2000	Jury member, 'Bouwkwaliteitsprijs', Rotterdam
2002	Jury member, 'Bouwkwaliteitsprijs', Rotterdam
2002–2006	Chairman, Committee of 'Welstand and Monumenten' Haarlemmermeer
2002–2006	Member of Stimuleringsfonds Architecture committee
2004	Jury member, BNA Kubus prize
2005	Member, RRKC, Rotterdam

Boris Zeisser

1968	Born in Alkmaar, The Netherlands
1989–1995	Technical University Delft, Faculty of Architecture (Honorable Mention)
1992	Min 2 Produkties, Bergen
1994	University of Illinois, Chicago, exchange program
1996–2000	(EEA) Erick van Egeraat Associated Architects, Rotterdam
2001–present	24H Architecture, Rotterdam

Teaching/Lectures

1996	Hogeschool voor de Kunsten, Utrecht
2004	Nova College, Haarlem
2006	University of Belfast, United Kingdom

Committees

2005	Jury member, Groninger Architectuurplrijs

CHRONOLOGY OF PROJECTS

2001	Ichthus Academy (extension), Rotterdam, The Netherlands
2001	Refurbishment of Amsterdamse School Villa, Zeist, The Netherlands
2001	Refurbishment of Doopgezinde Kerk (church), Purmerend, The Netherlands
2001	Urban study for Kennemer Gasthuis Terrein, Haarlem, The Netherlands
2001	Urban study for Sky Shuttle, Haaglanden, Den Haag, The Netherlands
2001	Urban plan for Kop van West, Purmerend, The Netherlands
2001–2002	Ichthus Academy, Rotterdam, The Netherlands
2001–2003	Housing (45 homes), Getsewoud, Nieuw Vennep, The Netherlands
2001–2003	Refurbishments of CWI offices, The Netherlands
2001–2004	Dragspelhuset (weekend house), Sweden
2002	Design for school, Haarlemmermeer, The Netherlands, (competition), 1st prize
2002	Multifunctional building, Slossberg, Böblingen, Germany, (competition)
2002	Pumpstation, Zeeburg, Amsterdam, The Netherlands (competition), second prize
2002	Study of Cinema Lantaarn/Venster, Rotterdam, The Netherlands
2002	Study of fitness centre for Beukenhorst, Hoofddorp, The Netherlands
2002	Study of offices for Beukenhorst Zuid, Hoofddorp, The Netherlands
2002	Study of private clinic for Parkkliniek, Rotterdam, The Netherlands
2002	Study of shop concept for Mart Visser, The Netherlands
2002	Study of shop concept for Mexx, The Netherlands
2002	Urban strategy for Baankwartier, Rotterdam, The Netherlands
2002	Urban study for Inholland Zuid-As, Amsterdam, The Netherlands
2002	Urban plan for Havenindustrie Terrein, Goes, The Netherlands
2002	Urban study for Randweg Noord, Hoofddorp, The Netherlands
2002	Urban study for Zeeburger Eiland (island), Amsterdam, The Netherlands
2002	Zorghotel, Hoofddorp, The Netherlands (competition), second prize
2002–2003	Lobby of Ashlee House Hotel, London, England
2002–2005	Study of ice pavilion for Haarlemmermeer, The Netherlands
2002–2007	Health and nature resort, Ardennen, Belgium
2002–2008	Housing, Gouwe, Waddinxveen, The Netherlands
2003	Beach pavilion, Sealand, Flanders, Belgium
2003	Housing, Schoterburcht, Haarlem, The Netherlands, (competition), 2nd prize

2003	Study for extension to the Europa School, Amsterdam, The Netherlands
2003	Study for shop concept, Tommy Hilfiger, Amsterdam, The Netherlands
2003	Urban study for Shell Terrein, Amsterdam, The Netherlands
2003–2004	Youth Club, Hoofddorp, The Netherlands
2003–2006	Housing (35 semi-detached houses and 60 social houses), Eiland 7 (Island 7), Floriande, Hoofddorp, The Netherlands
2004–2007	Housing (87 apartments), Sciencepark, Amsterdam, The Netherlands
2003–2008	Mixed-use complex, Van der Zee Lokatie, Hoofddorp
2004	Leisure centre, Zoetermeer, The Netherlands
2004	Urban study for Schutters Kwartier, Rotterdam, The Netherlands
2004–2005	Multifunctional complex, Aprisco, Hoofddorp, The Netherlands
2004–2005	Study for Beta Cluster, Uithof, Utrecht, The Netherlands
2004–2005	Study for fashion 'cave', Salzburg, Austria
2004–2006	Refurbishment of watertower, Domburg, The Netherlands
2004–2007	Refurbishment of spinnerij (spinning mill), Oosterveld, Enschede
2004–2007	Shops and housing (apartments), Blom Site, Hoofddorp, The Netherlands
2005	Arts Pavilion, Peckham, London, England, (competition), 2nd prize
2005	'Meesters van de Romantiek' (Romantic Movement) Exhibition, Kunsthal, Rotterdam, The Netherlands
2005	Study for holiday houses, Euro Disney, Paris, France
2005	Study for offices, Verlinden and Rittmeester, Den Bosch, The Netherlands
2005	Study for Uran, Smitsveen, Soest, The Netherlands
2005–2006	Sröborg Hadeland, Jevnaker, Norway
2005–2007	Business units, Moordrecht, The Netherlands
2005–2007	Courthouse Hostel, London, England
2005–2007	Co-housing (38 houses for musicians), Hoogvliet, The Netherlands
2005–2008	Housing (94 apartments) with commercial spaces, Hatert, Nijmegen, The Netherlands
2005–2008	Leisure centre and housing (60 apartments), Bodegraven, The Netherlands
2006	Dinosaurs in the Kunsthal Museum, Rotterdam, The Netherlands
2006	Eco-suite, Soneva Kiri Resort, Thailand
2006	Therman Spa, Boedha Sluis, The Netherlands
2006	Therman Spa, Mekka, Hoofddorp, The Netherlands
2006	Waldorf School (extension), Norrköping, Sweden

COLLABORATORS SINCE 2001

Heleen Bothof, Sabrina Kers, Suzanne Tóth-Pal, Rob Bothof,
Séverine Kas, Jeroen Ter Haar, Roos Kemna, Gerben Vos, Olav Bruin,
Fieke Poelman, Amelie Kaltenbach, Ingrid Owens, Sandra Vergin,
Mirjam van der Linde, Inge Dalmeijer, Penny Nourney, David Hess,
Wouter Homs, Casper de Heer, Blandine Roulet, Nora Rittmüller,
Susan Hoekstra, Sylvain Grasset, Ruben Bergambagt, Michele Stramezzi,
Saman Saffarian, Christian Schultze, Luzian Kohler, Sabine Simon,
Jacopo van der Horst, Sarah van Apeldoorn, Arnout Verweij,
Dirk Zschunke, Ben de Lange, Marie Allard-Latour, Sandor Marks,
Bruno Toledo, Petrine Arts, Christianne Schets, Marloes Swijnenburg,
Marta Koziol, Onat Oktem, Klasien Visser, Carlyn Timmermans,
Anne-Laure Nolan, Albert-Jan Vermeulen, Aggeliki Aggeli.

This publication was made possible
with the generous contribution of

Y'MERE
Door wonen gedreven

121

EMPLOYEES 2001-2006

Heleen Bothof, Rob Bothof, Olav Bruin, Inge Dalmeijer,
Sylvain Grasset, Jeroen ter Haar, Casper de Heer, Susan Hoekstra,
Wouter Homs, Amelie Kaltenbach, Séverine Kas, Roos Kemna,
Sabrina Kers, Mirjam van der Linde, Penny Nourney, Ingrid Owens,
Fieke Poelman, Blandine Roulet, Nora Rittmüller, Suzanne Tóth-Pal,
Sandra Vergin, Gerben Vos.

BIBLIOGRAPHY

Arts Pavilion

Stedebouw & Architectuur, The Netherlands, May 2005

Ashlee House Hostel

Maru, Korea, September 2003

Frame, United Kingdom, March 2004

C3, Korea, February 2005

Collidoscope, Laurence King Publishing, 2005

Baankwartier, Rotterdam

Algemeen dagblad, The Netherlands, September 2003

Beach Pavilions

Stedebouw & Architectuur, The Netherlands, May 2005

Dragspelhuset Summer House

Varmlands folkblad, Sweden, August 2002

Hout in de Bouw, The Netherlands, October 2002

Algemeen, The Netherlands, March 2003

Detail in Architectuur, The Netherlands, January 2003

Arvika Nyheter, Sweden, July 2003

Bouwwereld, The Netherlands, October 2003

De Architect, The Netherlands, November 2003

Forum, Sweden, November 2003

Frame, United Kingdom, January 2004

AIT, Germany, 2004

A+U, Japan, November 2003

De Architect, The Netherlands, February 2004

AMC, Le Moniteur, France, May 2004

Residence, Sweden, June 2004

Elle Decor, Italy, December 2004

Konstvärlden & Disajn, Sweden, 2004

Details, USA, March 2005

AW Architektur & Wettbewerbe, September 2004

Frame, United Kingdom, 2005

Abstract, Belgium, September 2004

View, The Netherlands, May 2004

NYA Wermlands-Tidningen, Sweden, August 2004

Architects Journal, United Kingdom, October 2004

Area, Italy, October 2004

Interior Design, USA, November 2004

Detail, Germany, December 2004

Elle Decor, France, December 2004

Elle Decoration, Germany, December 2004

Land, Sweden, September 2004

Architectures à Vivre, France, November/December 2004

Stedebouw & Architectuur, The Netherlands, May 2005

Casa la Repubblica, Italy, February 2005

The Sydney Morning Herald, Australia, January 2005

The Guardian, United Kingdom, December 2004

Il Giornale dell' Architettura, Italy, 2005

Metropolitan Home, USA, May 2005

C3, Korea, February 2005

Techniques & Architecture, France, February 2005

Bauwelt, Germany, January 2005

House and Leisure, January 2005

AD, Italy, December 2004

Eigen Huis en Interieur, The Netherlands, August 2005

Arkitekton, Italy, May 2005

Arquitectura Viva, Spain, July 2005

Woodlands Trust–Bark magazine, United Kingdom, summer 2005

Happinez, The Netherlands, September 2005

Pen magazine, Japan, January 2006

Volvo magazine, United Kingdom, February 2006

Atrium, Germany, February 2006

Dagbladet, Norway, July 2004

Case in Legno (Federico Motta Editore), September 2004

Tree Houses, Loft Publications, 2005

150 Best House Ideas, Loft Publications, 2005

50 Great Adventures, Prestel, 2005

Small Interiors, HK, 2005

Designing Public Toilets, Edizioni Gribaudo c/o Officina, 2005

TV1, Sweden, August 2004

HGTV, USA, January 2006

Konstmagasinet, Arvika, Sweden, 2003

Biblioteket, Arjang, Sweden, 2004

Getsewoud Housing

De Architect,The Netherlands, July, 2002

De Architect, The Netherlands, January 2003

Haarlems dagblad, The Netherlands, October 2003

AMC, Le Moniteur, France, May 2004

Stedebouw & Architectuur, The Netherlands, December 2004

New Appartments, Loft Publications, 2005

Hybrid housing for Musicians

De Telegraaf, February 2006

Ichthus Academie

AIT magazine, Germany, 2002

De Architect, The Netherlands, 2002

Domus, Italy, 2002

Zoo, United Kingdom, 2002

Frame, United Kingdom, August 2002

The Architectural Review, United Kingdom, September 2002

Elsevier Thema, The Netherlands, October 2002

Techniques & Architecture, France, 2002

C3, Korea, 228, August 2003

Maru, Korea, September 2003

A+U, Japan, November 2003

Diseño Interior, Spain, February 2004

Collidoscope, Laurence King Publishing, 2005

Ichthus Hogeschool

De Architect, The Netherlands, October 2003

Kop van West

Nieuwe Noordhollandse Courant, The Netherlands, February 2002

De Architect, The Netherlands, October 2003

Stedebouw & Architectuur, The Netherlands, May 2005

Multifunctional Building Böblingen

Stedebouw & Architectuur, The Netherlands, May 2005

Snow Castle

Forum, February 2006

Rotterdam's dagblad, The Netherlands, July 2002

Frame, United Kingdom, August 2002

De Architect, The Netherlands, September 2002

Art NL, The Netherlands, September 2002

The Art of Living, The Netherlands, October 2002

Elle Wonen, The Netherlands, November 2002

Spinning Mill

Urban Land Europe, United Kingdom, 2005

Watertower

Urban Land Europe, United Kingdom, 2005

PHOTOGRAPHY CREDITS

Christian Richters and 24H architecture.